CONTENTS

Welcome to the Y2K Time Machine

The 2000s were supposed to start with a bang. Remember Y2K? The global panic that convinced everyone that the stroke of midnight on December 31, 1999, would short-circuit every computer on Earth and send us spiraling back into the Stone Age? Planes would plummet, banks would implode, and, horror of horrors, Napster playlists would vanish. But when the ball dropped in Times Square, the lights stayed on. The world kept spinning. We entered a whole new millennium with all systems go—and what a ride the 2000s turned out to be!

Teen culture exploded louder than a boy-band chorus. Reality TV became *the* thing. Fashion embraced rhinestones and had a serious love affair with velour. Britney, Paris, and Lindsay weren't just names; they were forces of nature. The signoff "XOXO" was everywhere. But the 2000s weren't all glitter and gossip. We also saw movements that defined an era. Hip-hop didn't just rule the charts—it reshaped pop culture. Tolkien and Harry Potter turned bookworms into rock stars. And social media transformed from "that weird Internet thing" to an inescapable way of life.

Maybe the best parts of the 2000s weren't the big, flashy national headlines but the delightfully quirky moments that

TIME MACHINE TRIVIA

the 2000s

From Flip Phones and Frosted Tips to Reality TV and Robotic Pets, Hundreds of Nostalgic Facts from the Decade That Was So Fetch

WILLIAM LEE

BLUESTONE
BOOKS

TIME MACHINE TRIVIA: THE 2000S.

Published by:
Bluestone Books

www.bluestonebooks.co

ISBN: 978-1-965636-17-6 (paperback)
ISBN: 978-1-965636-22-0 (eBook)

Edited by Jennifer Calvert
Design by Joanna Williams

Printed in the United States of America

First Edition: 2025

10 9 8 7 6 5 4 3 2 1

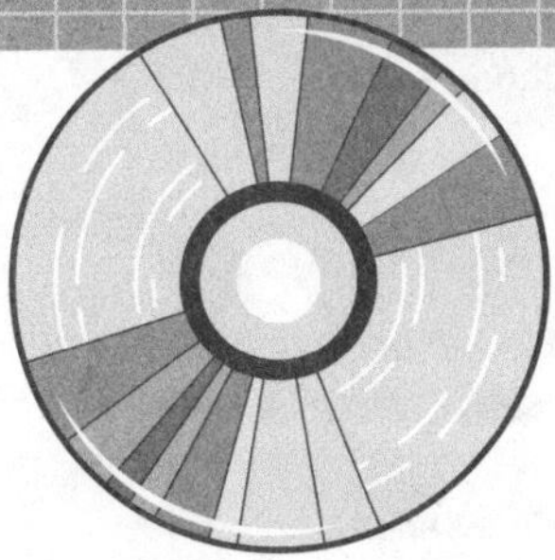

made the decade unforgettable: The awkward thrill of setting up your first MySpace profile and reveling in your "Top 8." The joy of unwrapping your first iPod—and spending hours loading it up. The pure chaos of choreographing a "Crank That" dance in your living room. An unexplainable attachment to robotic pets. The elevated view from platform shoes.

That's where *Time Machine Trivia* comes in. This book isn't just an archive of news reports from "the aughts." It brings you the hidden gems, the "Oh my gosh, I forgot about that!" moments, the *experiences* that made the decade special—and changed life ever after. So turn the page, and let's get this party started. The 2000s are calling . . . on their flip phone! And if you do hear a bang, it's just another Cha-Cha Slide collision on the dance floor.

"NOW I'M FEELIN' SO FLY LIKE A G6."

—Far East Movement, "Like a G6"

LOW-RISE JEANS and FROSTED DREAMS

Style Trendsetters and Trainwrecks

Jennifer Lopez redefined loungewear in 2001.

J.Lo traded traditional pop-star glitz for a hot pink Juicy Couture velour crop top and matching short-shorts in a music video, and suddenly, wearing sweats in public was no longer a fashion faux pas.

Juicy Couture skyrocketed thanks to celebrity exposure.

Lacking funds for traditional marketing, the founders gifted tracksuits to stars like Paris Hilton, Nicole Richie, Jessica Alba, and Eva Longoria. Their velour became an instant hit, and the founders proudly kept a photo wall of every celebrity who wore their brand.

Liz Claiborne (now Kate Spade & Company) acquired Juicy Couture in 2003.

The deal was $226 million, with payments spread over five years.

Britney Spears made tracksuits wedding-worthy.

At her wedding to Kevin Federline in 2004, Britney decked out her bridesmaids in bubblegum-pink Juicy tracksuits with "Maids" emblazoned on the back, while the groomsmen wore white tracksuits labeled "Pimps."

QUIZ

Which J.Lo music video debuted her Juicy look?

A. "Love Don't Cost a Thing"

B. "Waiting for Tonight"

C. "Let's Get Loud"

D. "I'm Real (Remix)"

Quiz Answer: D.

Ugg boots were suddenly everywhere in the aughts.

Although the clunky shearling-lined boots had been around since 1978, they shot to popularity and were spotted on the feet of many a fashionable woman in the early 2000s.

Oprah might have been responsible for this trend.

After the media mogul declared Uggs one of her "Favorite Things" in 2000, celebrities like Sarah Jessica Parker and Kate Moss started wearing them. (SJP deserved to wear something comfortable after so many hours in stilettos.)

Uggs ushered in the start of a much more comfortable era.

Juicy Couture with Uggs became a popular combination, marking the beginning of America's obsession with loungewear as clothing.

The boots were originally beachwear.

Early Ugg boots were worn by surfers in Australia to keep their feet warm in between sessions. They were designed for men, but the surfers' girlfriends started "borrowing" them. From there, it was a short jump to seeing celebs sporting them around Hollywood.

The brand has always been in on the joke—Ugg is short for ugly.

Australians are known for shortening (sometimes already short) words. Sunglasses are sunnies, breakfast is brekkie, and ugly boots are uggies.

Paris Hilton was the medieval princess of unexpected fashion trends.

When Paris Hilton showed up to her twenty-first birthday party in 2002 wearing a glittery and drapey silver dress made from chain-mail mesh, it made waves instantly.

The chain-mail mini-dress went mainstream after Paris's party.

Fashion idols like Naomi Campbell and Kate Moss and music icons like Beyoncé and Rihanna sported similar slinky metal-mesh outfits.

Supermodel Kendall Jenner paid homage to Hilton's style in 2016.

Jenner wore a recreation of Hilton's chain-mail dress to her own twenty-first birthday party in 2016, cementing it in fashion history.

Kendall isn't the only member of the Kardashian clan with ties to Paris Hilton.

Hilton hired then-stylist Kim Kardashian as her personal assistant in 2006, just one year before her new employee rose to infamy, then fame, with the leak of her sex tape.

QUIZ

Which of the following looks did Paris Hilton *not* rock in front of the paparazzi?

A. White bucket hat

B. Grateful Dead dress

C. Low-cut jeans

D. Tiaras

Quiz Answer: Paris wore it all.

The fashion industry embraced luxury brands in the 2000s.

After the big colors and bold choices of the 1980s, fashion went back to basics in the 1990s. Stores like Gap and Banana Republic featured primary colors, simplicity, and functionality. By the 2000s, people were ready for another shift. The reaction was fierce: minimalism gave way to maximalism.

"Logomania" went mainstream after Y2K.

Why spend hundreds or thousands of dollars on a Fendi tote if nobody could tell what it was? Throughout the 1990s, designers like Dapper Dan had been making custom outfits splashed with luxury-brand logos for many big-name rappers. By the 2000s, everyday people were displaying the logos of their clothing and accessories as much as possible. Many brands responded to the trend by emphasizing their logos.

People clamored for brands like Gucci, Chanel, and Louis Vuitton.

Those logos were some of the most frequently seen and most prominently displayed on clothing and handbags in the 2000s. We're talking large, bold lettering that was placed in multiple locations on each item.

Brands that didn't give in to logomania fell behind.

Companies like Burberry that bet on "timeless luxury" and subtly recognizable designs lost big once logomania took hold.

The real Von Dutch had nothing to do with fashion.

Kenneth "Von Dutch" Howard was a mechanic, auto detailer, and artist who made a name customizing hot rods in California. After his death in 1992, art collector Ed Boswell, former drug dealer Michael Cassel, and competitive surfer Bobby Vaughn came together to build his name into a somewhat garage-centric fashion brand with only a passing connection to its source.

Christian Audigier made Von Dutch what it was.

After the French designer came on board in 2002, he pushed the brand into a trendier and more celebrity-focused direction. Sales took off right away.

It was all about the hat.

When Von Dutch introduced the trademark trucker hat, which retailed for as much as $125, it became a must-have item among celebrities like Jay-Z, Madonna, Britney Spears, and Paris Hilton.

QUIZ

Which celebrity was known for wearing Von Dutch hats on their show?

A. Spencer Pratt, *The Hills*

B. Tyra Banks, *America's Next Top Model*

C. Nicole Richie, *The Simple Life*

D. Ashton Kutcher, *Punk'd*

Quiz Answer: D.

The brand's downfall happened fast.

The brand was sold off in 2009 and lived on as something of a punch line about mindless trendoids. (One memorable nickname: "Von Douche.")

Trendsetter Don Ed Hardy started out as a tattoo artist.

Hardy helped popularize dense and colorful Japanese tattooing styles in America while running his own tattoo parlor in San Francisco in the late 1970s.

Von Dutch's Christian Audigier turned Don Ed Hardy into "Ed Hardy."

The French denim designer created the brand; slapped Hardy's baroque, rainbow-hued designs onto every bit of clothing he could; and aggressively marketed it to celebrities with a slathering of rhinestones and sequins.

Ed Hardy clothes were described as "tattoo lifestyle."

They featured skulls, roses, and phrases like "love kills slowly." Celebrities such as David Beckham and Madonna bought the stuff by the (very expensive) truckload.

Jon Gosselin's love of Ed Hardy turned the tide on the brand.

When the so-called "villain" of reality show *Jon & Kate Plus 8*, who often wore the brand's clothes, was photographed on Audigier's yacht with his new girlfriend in 2009, clubs actually started banning people who wore Ed Hardy clothes.

Hardy sued Audigier.

Ed Hardy the brand was pulling in $700 million a year by 2009, but Ed Hardy the man was not. He filed a lawsuit, alleging that Audigier underreported sales and underpaid Hardy's royalties.

Tattoos became just another fashion accessory.

Once aughts fashion decreed that women needed to show as much midriff as possible (heralded by low-rise jeans and crop tops), the race was on to accessorize the belly. Midriff tats accompanied belly-button piercings and studded belts.

Britney Spears was a big fan of expressive ink.

Some of the pop singer's early tattoos included a blonde fairy with pink wings on her lower back, the Chinese symbol for "strange" (she had wanted it to say "mysterious") on her hip, pink dice on her left wrist to match then-husband Kevin Federline's blue ones on his right wrist, and a triangle on her right hand between her thumb and index finger.

QUIZ

In which movie did Vince Vaughn's character say, "Tattoo on the lower back? Might as well be a bull's-eye."

A. *The Break-Up* (2006)

B. *Wedding Crashers* (2005)

C. *Couples Retreat* (2009)

D. *Fred Claus* (2007)

Quiz Answer: B.

Tattoos even got their own reality shows.

The first unscripted show featuring tattoo artists premiered on TLC in 2005. *Miami Ink* followed the misadventures of local tattoo artists and their customers, which included celebrities like Anthony Bourdain and Bam Margera. Multiple spinoffs followed, set in Los Angeles, London, Madrid, and New York.

Heelys rolled out in December 2000.

The first store that carried the hybrid sneakers with a removable wheel in the sole sold out in hours. Equal parts footwear and lifestyle, Heelys defined effortlessly cool rebellion—especially when schools began banning them.

Features on the skate shoes appeared in magazines from *People* to *Wired*.

Usher rocked them on stage. And the brand built six pairs for NBA star Shaquille O'Neal.

For the comfort crowd, Crocs were unveiled at the Fort Lauderdale Boat Show in 2002.

Originally designed as boat shoes, Crocs made their way onto land and into the closets of chefs, nurses, gardeners, and public figures like Jennifer Garner, Oprah Winfrey, and Michelle Obama.

The creators of 2006's *Idiocracy* couldn't imagine Crocs catching on.

Cowriter Mike Judge admitted they'd intentionally chosen the unknown and unconventional brand for their dystopian comedy. They filmed in 2004, and by 2005, Crocs were selling in the millions and being sported by celebrities.

The little decorative charms that fit in the holes of Crocs are called Jibbitz.

Designers Sheri and Rich Schmelzer sold Jibbitz to Crocs for $10 million in 2006.

The bohemian look came back with a vengeance in the 2000s.

What started as an artsy, free-spirited style in the late 1800s—think flowy fabrics, scarves, and a dash of European flair—made a splash in the 1970s with icons like Stevie Nicks and Jane Birkin. It reemerged in the 2000s on red carpets and sidewalks alike, with tiered skirts, fringe bags, and oversized sunglasses.

Cameron Crowe's '70s rock-star movie *Almost Famous* (2000) gave "boho chic" a push.

The film gave Kate Hudson her breakout role as the captivating "band aid" (*not* "groupie") Penny Lane. Her giant sunglasses, fur-trimmed coats, miniskirts, flowing blouses, and flared trousers set the boho chic template for a new generation.

Celebrities jumped on board fast.

Style setters like Kate Moss and Nicole Richie turned the secondhand look into first-rate fashion, while singer Joss Stone brought flower-child vibes to award shows. On *Gossip Girl*, Blake Lively's Serena van der Woodsen made "Upper East Side boho" a thing.

Sienna Miller was key to the movement.

Though relatively unknown in the United States for her movie work, the British actress became a boho-chic style maven in the 2000s due largely to widely disseminated pictures of her in big sunglasses, boho accessories, and—of course—Uggs at the massive Glastonbury music festival in 2004.

The Victoria's Secret Fashion Show went prime time in 2001.

First launched in 1995 to showcase the brand's latest lingerie, the VS Fashion Show mixed high-fashion runway vibes with plenty of sex appeal aimed squarely at the *Maxim* crowd. After experimenting with webcasts in the late '90s, the show leveled up in 2001, strutting straight into ABC's prime-time lineup and millions of living rooms.

Heidi Klum wore a bra priced at $12.5 million.

The lingerie extravaganza was held in New York's Bryant Park, which also hosts Fashion Week, and had several standout moments, such as Andrea Bocelli's appearance and the jewel-encrusted "Fantasy Bra." All the new-millennium models were there, from Klum to Gisele Bündchen and Tyra Banks.

America's Next Top Model premiered in 2003.

Supermodels like Naomi Campbell, Claudia Schiffer, and Kate Moss were *so* '90s. Though they remained style magnates, the 2000s were about finding the up-and-coming models.

QUIZ

Which model said, "I lost a trillion-dollar bracelet on the runway. I have no idea where it went"?

A. Gisele Bündchen
B. Alessandra Ambrosio
C. Tyra Banks
D. Heidi Klum

Quiz Answer: C.

America's Next Top Model first premiered on UPN.

When *American Idol* exploded in 2002, networks scrambled to duplicate its success. The next year, *ANTM* premiered on UPN, a struggling network that needed a breakout hit. The series was a mash-up of an *Idol*-style competition show with the *Real World*-ish bickering that comes from throwing fame-hungry youths into shared living quarters while producers instigate conflict to create "characters."

Tyra Banks was to *ANTM* as Simon Cowell was to *Idol*.

Among the judges in "Cycle 1" were former models Janice Dickinson and Kimora Lee Simmons. But the face of the show was Banks. She delivered a mix of feedback to contestants that ranged from confidence-inspiring speeches to cutting critiques.

UPN merged with The WB to become The CW in 2006.

By 2010, *ANTM* was still going strong on the new channel. Some judges came (like Twiggy and André Leon Talley) while others went (like Simmons), but Tyra remained.

Tyra coined many a phrase for the show.

The catchphrases Tyra tried *very hard* to inject into the culture through constant repetition included:

- **Dreckitude:** No good.
- **Fierce:** Not exactly hers, but she tried very hard to own it.
- **H2T:** From head to toe.
- **Smize:** Smiling with your eyes rather than your lips.

The fashion reality boomlet continued with *Project Runway*.

Bravo, a basic cable channel that presented somewhat more artistic fare than, say, TLC, launched this show in 2004. The premise, in which up-and-coming designers compete to make the best clothes under specific constraints, was focused on fashion like *ANTM* but also on expertise.

Audiences came to discover the genius of Tim Gunn.

The face of *Project Runway* was supermodel Heidi Klum, but the real star was her cohost, Tim Gunn. An educator with a long tenure at different fashion schools, he served as the quietly supportive advisor who drifted from one designer to another, providing helpful tips as they frantically worked against the clock.

Project Runway became must-see viewing for fashionistas.

The list of winners who became big successes after being on the show with Klum and Gunn is surprisingly short. Still, the show gained respect from the industry, largely for its emphasis on craft, and earned its own slot at New York Fashion Week.

QUIZ

Which of the following designers hit it big after being on *Project Runway*?

A. Keith Michael
B. Christian Siriano
C. Jasmine Chong
D. Isaac Saqib

Quiz Answer: B.

Graphic T-shirts were everywhere.

From "I'm with Stupid" to "Save Ferris" and "That's Hot," comfy tees had a unique way of tapping into the zeitgeist—whatever it was at that moment.

The 2004 surprise hit *Napoleon Dynamite* spawned "Vote for Pedro" tees.

In the goofy indie comedy, a gawky high school kid makes "Vote for Pedro" T-shirts to help get his (also gawky) friend Pedro elected as student body president. Hot Topic produced the real thing, which became its most popular tee ever.

Skateboard label Supreme tried to ride Calvin Klein's coattails.

In the mid-2000s, Supreme's founder, James Jebbia, and his team started slapping brand stickers on Calvin Klein underwear ads featuring Kate Moss around New York City. Eventually, Supreme went ahead and made a T-shirt from the ad. Their guerrilla marketing got them sued.

British patriotism made an unexpectedly Zen comeback.

"Keep Calm and Carry On" was originally a British government slogan from 1939 meant to boost morale as World War II loomed. But, in the 2000s, this stiff-upper-lip motto had a staggering second life across the pond on American T-shirts and posters.

Etsy started as a Brooklyn-based maker-friendly market for handmade goods.

Rob Kalin, Chris Maguire, and Haim Schoppik founded Etsy in 2005. The simple functionality and open-door policy, welcoming all kinds of artisanal creations, helped sellers easily craft their own online commerce sites.

Etsy started slow, then boomed.

In May 2006, the site generated $170,000 in sales. A year later, that number had multiplied by a factor of ten as artisans joined Etsy in droves to sell their homemade soaps, ironic T-shirts, and other handcrafted goods.

The site became less artisanal in 2008.

That was the year Maguire and Schoppik left; Kalin stayed on but stepped back from the day-to-day as the site expanded to compete with eBay and other online marketplaces selling drop-shipped items and printables.

"Regretsy" gathered the worst of the website for everyone's schadenfreude.

In 2009, voice actor April Winchell started this satirical site with the slogan "Where DIY Meets WTF" to celebrate and viciously mock all the worst things that could be found on Etsy. A book of the same name followed in 2010.

QUIZ

Which item *wasn't* featured on Regretsy?

A. Crocheted Beanie Baby sling

B. Double hummingbird-feeder hat

C. Chicken poncho

D. Lady Gaga embroidered toilet paper

Quiz Answer: A.

Lance Armstrong was America's first cycling influencer.

The Tour de France winner returned to racing a few years after his 1996 cancer diagnosis, winning the prestigious race seven consecutive times and turning his recovery into an against-the-odds story that captivated people who normally would never care about bike racing.

His Livestrong bracelets became a must-have fashion accessory.

Armstrong's cancer support nonprofit, the Livestrong Foundation, partnered with Nike to raise money and awareness through their bright yellow silicone bracelets, which the cyclist introduced on *TODAY* in 2004. They became so popular that both George W. Bush and John Kerry wore them during the presidential election that year.

The bracelets were a fundraising machine.

The foundation pulled in over $100 million of funding for cancer research and survivor support, largely due to the bracelets. (Numbers fell off after Armstrong admitted to doping in 2013.)

Other charities picked up on the idea.

Pretty soon, silicone bracelets of different hues were raising awareness for a whole range of issues. The Susan G. Komen Foundation went all in on pink bracelets for breast cancer awareness before pivoting to Panera's Pink Ribbon Bagel (introduced in 2001).

The people behind Livestrong bracelets also made Sillybandz.

Entrepreneur and novelty toymaker Robert Croak jumped on the coattails of the Livestrong bracelet trend. He was at a trade show in China in 2007 when he saw skinny silicone-rubber wristbands that could be molded into different shapes. He brought the idea home with him and had his company whip something up.

Sillybandz went on sale in 2008.

The cheap, colorful wristbands had one gimmick: when you took them off your wrist, they snapped back into a preexisting shape—usually an animal. Almost immediately, consumers bought them by the thousands.

Sales peaked in 2010.

That year, Croak's company sold a truly astonishing $200 million worth of Sillybandz. They came in hundreds of different styles, which were briskly traded by schoolchildren (before promptly being banned in many schools).

Puka-shell necklaces had another moment in the sun.

These Hawaiian creations were part of a short craze in the 1970s that returned in the early 2000s.

QUIZ

Which popular 2000s TV show helped the puka-shell craze along?

A. *Supernatural*

B. *The Office*

C. *The O.C.*

D. *Charmed*

Quiz Answer: C.

"TECHNOLOGY,
LIKE ANYTHING ELSE
THAT MANKIND CREATES,
IS A TOOL, AND THAT TOOL
CAN BE USED FOR GOOD
OR FOR EVIL, LIKE A
LIGHT SABER."

—RAINN WILSON

FROM DIAL-UP to DOWNLOAD

The Tech That Changed Our Lives

The PS2 became the best-selling video game console in history in 2000.

The 1990s were a great time for gamers, with the move from 2D to 3D making video games more immersive. But Sony's PlayStation 2 changed everything. It played DVDs, had an Internet connection and incredible graphics, and was backward compatible.

PlayStation pushed Sega out of the hardware business.

Sony released the PS2 not long after Sega released their Dreamcast, which was meant to be a category killer. After that, Sega got out of the hardware business to focus on its gaming franchises, like *Sonic the Hedgehog*.

The designer-friendly PS2 cornered the market on games.

Pretty soon, it had more games than any other console out there, topping out at more than 4,000. Huge franchises like *Grand Theft Auto*, *Final Fantasy*, *Metal Gear*, and *Gran Turismo* ensured that gamers never ran out of things to race or shoot.

Sony killed their own momentum with the pricey PS3.

When Sony put out the PS3 in 2006, the idea was to go bigger and better, with massive processing power, Blu-ray storage, and better resolution than anything else on the market. But after seeing the $500 (and up) price tag, many PS2 owners opted not to upgrade.

Microsoft broke out of the computer box and into the console world in 2001.

That November, Microsoft launched the Xbox to challenge Sony's PlayStation 2. The console featured advanced graphics, cutting-edge sound, and a built-in hard drive.

"The Duke" was the popular nickname for the controller.

It had a giant X in the middle that looked over-the-top 2000s cool but did absolutely nothing.

The Xbox was a "sixth-generation" video game console.

The sixth generation of video game consoles generally includes the years 1998 through 2004 and consoles like Sega Dreamcast (1998), Sony PlayStation 2 (2000), and Nintendo GameCube (2001).

QUIZ

How much was the release price of the original Xbox?

A. $199

B. $299

C. $399

D. $499

Quiz Answer: B.

You were likely to find *Halo* and *Dead or Alive 3* in any Xbox household.

Halo was originally slated to be a PC game, but Microsoft grabbed it up for Xbox.

Xbox Live changed the game by bringing players together.

In November 2002, Microsoft introduced the broadband multiplayer service that connected gamers around the world.

Handheld gaming took off in the 2000s.

While video game consoles that connected to TVs proliferated in the 2000s, companies were simultaneously moving ahead with developing portable games.

Sony and Nintendo went head-to-head in 2004.

With its touch screen and stylus, the Nintendo DS was a big step up from the company's popular Gameboy Advance. Sony pushed back with their first handheld, the PlayStation Portable (PSP).

The DS won out.

The PSP had more power and better graphics, but the DS was cheaper, was better for casual gamers, and had a bigger library of games to choose from. It went on to sell more than twice as many units as the PSP.

While handheld gaming grew, sales of physical games dropped.

In 2004, Valve launched its highly anticipated game *Half-Life 2* in a then-revolutionary way: to play it, buyers had to subscribe to the developer's new online platform, Steam. By the end of the 2000s, gamers were getting games, updates, and community from Steam and declining to buy physical copies.

QUIZ

What ill-conceived slogan did Nintendo use to market its DS?

A. "Touching is good."

B. "Stroke your screen."

C. "Feel the pixels."

D. "It likes when you tap it."

Quiz Answer: A.

The Wii (pronounced "Whee!") cornered the console market in 2006.

It's hard to overstate what a huge deal the Nintendo Wii was. The N64 and GameCube weren't exactly smashes, but Nintendo regained their mid-1990s mojo with this new console.

Nintendo's winning strategy? Simplicity, fun, and a lack of sticker shock.

The $249.99 Wii stayed out of the Xbox–PlayStation competition over who had better graphics and processing power. Instead, it came with a motion-sensitive controller that looked like a TV remote and could act like a tennis racket, gun, or baseball bat, among other things.

People who never played video games liked the Wii.

Nintendo's $200 million marketing blitz made everybody aware of the Wii. The approachable console came bundled with one game, *Wii Sports*, which was as different from the grim first-person shooters and arcane fantasy mythologies proliferating on other consoles as you could imagine. The so-called "casual gamer" market exploded.

They even used Wii to exercise.

One of the bestselling games of the late 2000s was *Wii Fit*, which came with a balance board that captured whole-body movement. And *Wii Sports*'s bowling feature was a hit in retirement homes.

Before there was Facebook, there was Friendster.

Canadian programmer Jonathan Abrams started Friendster (its name is a play on that of the music site Napster) in March of 2002 so people could make connections through mutual friends, build communities around shared tastes, and post photos. By fall of that year, Friendster already had 3 million users.

Abrams turned down Google.

Abrams turned down a $30 million stock offer from Google in 2003. He then brought in venture capital investors, who installed a board of directors that ended up ousting Abrams as CEO in 2004. If Abrams had taken Google's stock offer, he would have been worth $1 billion in the early 2020s.

Google tried—and failed—to get revenge.

The search company started a rival networking site, Orkut, in 2004. (It was big in Brazil.)

The new board ran Friendster into the ground.

The company's obituaries were already being written as early as 2005 thanks to a poor interface, reluctance to innovate, and a user base that had mostly migrated overseas and stopped using the site. It eventually suspended service in 2015.

QUIZ

Which of these was *not* a real early social-networking site?

A. ConnectU
B. NearBy
C. Six Degrees
D. Classmates

Quiz Answer: B.

MySpace launched in August of 2003.

The site had most of the benefits of Friendster (checking in with friends, finding dates, posting pictures). But it stood apart by allowing users to customize their profiles, which people did in droves, littering the site with online versions of their bedroom walls.

"MySpace Tom" was a friend to everyone.

MySpace automatically gave every new user a starter friend: Tom Anderson, one of MySpace's cofounders. This meant that Tom's profile picture (an innocuous shot of a short-haired young guy with a big grin) was one of the most widely seen images in the world for a time.

Adele landed a record deal after an executive saw her demos on MySpace.

The site gained popularity in large part due to its focus on music. Bands could essentially use MySpace as a free website to connect with fans, stream their music, and promote their shows.

News Corporation bought MySpace in 2005.

The price was $580 million.

By 2006, MySpace dominated the social-networking landscape.

The site was responsible for 80 percent of social-network site traffic that year. In 2007, it had over 300 million users. But MySpace couldn't keep up with emerging competition.

Social media as we know it today started as a dorm-room project.

On February 4, 2004, Mark Zuckerberg and his roommates launched TheFacebook—a social-networking site initially restricted to Harvard students.

At first, Facebook was exclusive to college students.

Facebook (dropping "The" from its name) soon expanded to universities beyond Harvard. Then, on September 1, 2005, it opened its virtual doors to high-school students. On September 26, 2006, anyone over thirteen with an email address could join the party.

The News Feed gave birth to scrolling.

Facebook's introduction of the News Feed feature in September 2006 turned profiles into a live stream of photos, posts, and updates. The update revolutionized how people consumed and shared information online.

Gaming came into the social media mix in 2007.

With the birth of Facebook Platform came hits like FarmVille and Mafia Wars, turning Facebook friends into gaming rivals.

Facebook Chat enabled the original "DM me."

The messaging feature gave users the option to move comments from public posts to a private space in 2008. It evolved into the Messenger app in 2011.

It was five years before Facebook launched its iconic "Like" button.

In February 2009, Facebook revealed one of its most defining features: the simple thumbs-up icon. It quickly became a popular tool for interacting with posts and photos and an easy way to say, "Yeah, I saw that."

Facebook grew exponentially in its first few years.

In 2004, the site had an impressive 1 million active users. In 2006, it had 12 million. By 2008, it boasted 100 million. And by the end of the aughts, the site had an incredible 608 million users (about half of what it had by 2024).

David Fincher's *The Social Network* gave a dark take on Facebook's founding.

Based on Ben Mezrich's book *The Accidental Billionaires*, this 2010 drama written by Aaron Sorkin portrayed Mark Zuckerberg (played by Jesse Eisenberg) as a brilliant and driven yet petty, vindictive, and socially awkward narcissist. In the movie, Zuckerberg creates a site called "Facemash" to rank hacked pictures of female Harvard students according to their attractiveness after getting dumped by his girlfriend.

QUIZ

What was Mark Zuckerberg's response to *The Social Network*'s take on him?

A. "Loved it!"

B. "No comment."

C. "Kind of hurtful."

D. "Eisenberg was great."

Quiz Answer: C.

Twitter got its start from a floundering podcast start-up.

When Apple launched iTunes podcasting in 2005, podcast start-up Odeo went back to the drawing board. That's when one of their Web designers, Jack Dorsey, floated the idea of being able to share your "status." Dorsey and three colleagues called the project "Twttr."

At first, Twitter was like group texting.

First released on July 15, 2006, Twttr let you text one number (40404) and send that message (in 140 characters or less) to a select group of friends.

An earthquake changed everything.

Most early adopters of Twttr were techies talking to each other about mundane stuff. That changed after an earthquake hit San Francisco in August 2006 and people realized Twttr was handy for quick info blasts during a crisis.

SXSW made Twitter a thing.

Newly rebranded Twitter found its footing at the March 2007 South by Southwest tech conference in Austin, Texas. Usage boomed from 20,000 to 60,000 messages (later called "tweets") per day.

Hashtags changed everything.

An ever-growing number of tweets flying around the system caused chaos. Then, in August 2007, tech entrepreneur Chris Messina introduced the idea of organizing tweets around subjects or channels by using the pound (#) sign.

Twitter's "Fail Whale" made waiting just a little better.

Twitter was still a small operation when it started taking off, so the service would sometimes get overwhelmed. When that happened, users saw a "Twitter is over capacity" message accompanied by a drawing of a cute beluga whale being carried above a rough sea by several orange birds.

Facebook became a copycat when Twitter's popularity spiked in the late 2000s.

Facebook replicated Twitter's status-update feature, hashtags, and "retweeting" function.

On April 17, 2009, Ashton Kutcher became the first Twitter user to hit 1 million followers.

The onetime host of *Punk'd* challenged CNN to a followers race, pledging that if he won, he would ding-dong-ditch the home of network founder Ted Turner. Instead, he brought 800 boxes of Ding Dongs to Turner's restaurant.

QUIZ

What did Jack Dorsey's first tweet say?

A. "facebook sux"
B. "help"
C. "hi"
D. "just setting up my twttr"

Quiz Answer: D.

Obama beat Kutcher to the boards.

Though Kutcher got all the glory, Barack Obama beat him to Twitter by over a year, sending his first tweet in April 2007. Britney Spears, Lady Gaga, and Taylor Swift also started tweeting before Kutcher.

Microsoft's founder, Bill Gates, was the target of a lot of anti-PC hate.

Though he looked and sounded like the quiet systems-admin guy at many people's companies, his immense power, gargantuan wealth, and hardball business tactics made some people suspect that his geeky persona was just a veneer for villainy.

Two movies supposedly modeled their villains on Bill Gates.

In 2001's *Antitrust*, Tim Robbins plays Gary Winston, a multi-billionaire tech CEO with a Gates-like haircut and murderously malicious way of dealing with the competition. The following year's *Clockstoppers* saw Michael Biehn play an evil tech CEO named *Henry* Gates. (Must be a coincidence.)

Microsoft killed off its quirky virtual assistant in Office 2007.

Gates wasn't the only one with a bad rap. Mention "Clippy" to old Windows users, and you might see signs of aggravation. The paper-clip avatar used to answer queries in Office programs. But people found his incessant interruptions so infuriating that Microsoft finally laid him to rest.

A Microsoft exec once admitted he'd rather have a Mac.

In a 2004 email that came to light during an antitrust case against Microsoft, Jim Allchin wrote, "I would buy a Mac today if I was not working at Microsoft."

Apple made computers fun again.

The company was revered as a scrappy and brilliant upstart that innovated, blazed trails, and changed how people saw computers.

Apple's Steve Jobs seemed like the anti-Gates.

Compared with Bill Gates's nerdy vibes and generic beige computers outfitted with accounting software, Jobs seemed like some kind of mysterious ex-hippie who made beautiful machines. In *Star Wars* terms, Jobs was portrayed as Han Solo to Gates's unnamed imperial officer standing next to Darth Vader.

QUIZ

What did Bono once call Apple?

A. "A religious cult"

B. "A fun company"

C. "Our number one fan"

D. "Not as cool as they think"

Quiz Answer: A.

Macs were aspirational.

Apple only ever had a relatively small share of the personal computer market—people used PCs at work because that's what their companies bought. But those people often dreamed of having their own sleek or colorful iMacs.

Apple billed themselves as the *cool* guys.

Leaning into the stereotypes, the company ran a ubiquitous ad campaign from 2006 to 2009 called "Get a Mac" that pitted Justin Long's cool and casual Mac against John Hodgman's stuffy, spreadsheet-loving PC in a suit and tie.

Google became the world's most widely used Internet search engine in 2000.

Earlier sites like Altavista and Ask Jeeves just couldn't cut it.

It didn't take long for "Google" to become a verb.

In a 2002 *Buffy the Vampire Slayer* episode, one character asks another, "Have you Googled her yet?" The word entered the *Oxford English Dictionary* in 2006 as a verb (transitive, in case you were curious).

People thought Gmail was literally too good to be true.

When Google announced their free email service, complete with 1 GB of storage, on April 1, 2004, many thought it was an April Fool's Day joke. That first iteration didn't even have a delete button—with so much free space, there was no need to clean out your inbox. *Ever.*

To be fair, Google loved a good April Fool's gag.

In 2000, they joked that they'd created a search engine called MentalPlex, powered by people projecting images of what they were looking for. In 2007, they "launched" TiSP (Toilet Internet Service Provider), which required connecting a fiber-optic cable and router in the sewer system. In 2010, they announced they were changing the company's name to "Topeka."

Pets.com was the poster child for the dot-com bubble.

The site roared into the new millennium with a big IPO in February 2000, only to go bankrupt later that year.

They did zero market research and lost money on every sale.

Even kitschy Internet companies with catchy ad campaigns featuring a snarky singing sock puppet needed a functional business plan.

The company was ahead of its time.

Unlike customers today, early-aughts shoppers simply weren't willing to wait for their pet supplies when they could easily run out to their neighborhood store.

The agency that created the sock puppet later got sued over the Taco Bell chihuahua.

In 2003, two artists sued Taco Bell for stealing their "psycho chihuahua" concept for the "Yo Quiero Taco Bell" ads and won $42 million. Although Taco Bell execs took the stolen idea to Pets.com sock-puppet creator TBWA Chiat/Day themselves, the fast-food company turned around and sued the ad agency for using it.

QUIZ

Which soft-rock band performed the song that was crooned by the Pets.com sock puppet?

A. Chicago
B. Fleetwood Mac
C. REO Speedwagon
D. The Eagles

Quiz Answer: A.

The first podcast released with zero fanfare.

In 2003, software developer Dave Winer and journalist Christopher Lydon recorded a conversation they held at Harvard. Winer turned the audio into a downloadable MP3 file and posted it on the Internet. And lo, the basic technology that made possible every true crime or football podcast you've ever listened to was launched.

Podcasting was almost called "audioblogging."

Talking about this boom time for "amateur radio" in 2004, the *Guardian*'s Ben Hammersley threw out some potential monikers. "Podcasting" stuck. "Audioblogging" did not.

A 1980s icon became a 2000s podcasting pioneer.

Onetime MTV VJ Adam Curry (the one with the massive halo of hair who hosted metal fest *Headbangers Ball*) started a radio show called *Daily Source Code* in 2004 with Dave Winer. They talked music, media, and software on what turned into the first daily podcast.

Apple got on board.

The company placed a bet on the medium's future success by building full podcast support into the 2005 release of iTunes 4.9. Steve Jobs called podcasting "TiVO for radio" (a comparison that makes little sense today).

Brad Fitzpatrick was looking for a challenge when he started LiveJournal.

The self-taught coder added his personal online journal to his website as a way to play with his skills and connect with his friends. He had so much fun with it that he created LiveJournal and opened it to the public.

Part blog, part social-networking site, LiveJournal took off in the 2000s.

People posted everything to the site, from heartfelt album reviews to mundane updates and celebrity gossip. ("Oh No They Didn't!" was one of the most popular communities.)

Emo status updates? LiveJournal invented them.

The site once had a "Current Mood" drop-down with over 130 options—including "accomplished," "bouncy," and the ever-useful "quixotic."

George R. R. Martin's first tweet in 2014 was a plug for his LiveJournal.

LiveJournal may have peaked in 2005 with 2.5 million active accounts, but some users (like Martin) stayed with it for far longer than most.

QUIZ

Which of the following was *not* a free blogging site in the early 2000s?

A. Blogspot
B. Medium
C. Wordpress
D. Xanga

Quiz Answer: B.

Tumblr became everyone's preferred online pastime in 2007.

Launched by twenty-one-year-old Web developer David Karp, it quickly became the Internet's favorite place to reblog fan art, scream about TV shows, and argue over which color "aesthetic" you were.

It didn't even have a reblog button.

In the early days of Tumblr, you had to manually copy and paste posts to share them. The site added the reblog feature in late 2007, and "reblog if you agree" and "reblog for good luck" posts were a steady thing by 2009—often featuring pixel-art bunnies, broken hearts, or mysterious curses. Tumblr was spooky *and* sentimental.

Fandoms helped Tumblr hit its first big user boom in 2010.

Entire dashboards erupted over shipping wars, headcanons, and emotionally devastating fan edits about *Glee*, *Sherlock*, and *Harry Potter*.

Yahoo! swore they wouldn't screw up Tumblr.

When announcing their acquisition of Tumblr for $1.1 billion in 2013, the Web conglomerate stated, "Per the agreement and our promise not to screw it up, Tumblr will be independently operated as a separate business." (Spoiler alert: they screwed it up.)

Per *Merriam-Webster*, "blog" was the most looked-up word in the dictionary in 2004.

They added it to their print dictionary in 2005.

"Mommy bloggers" became a powerful force in 2002.

Parenting blogs quickly gained an audience with their highly personal and sometimes product-driven narratives about child-rearing. Their creators have since been referred to as "the original influencers."

QUIZ

What were the Weblog Awards known as?

A. Blogsters
B. Dundies
C. Webbies
D. Bloggies

Quiz Answer: D.

Blogging got political in 2004.

That's the year political blogs were considered influential enough to earn their creators press credentials for the Democratic and Republican national conventions.

Dooce provided a cautionary tale about social media.

Users coined the term "dooced" in 2002 to describe what happened to Heather Armstrong, who was fired after complaining about her day job on her blog, *Dooce*.

Google bought Blogger in 2005.

Combined with already-owned Blogspot, it became one of the most widely used platforms and helped Google corner the market on blogs.

Celebrity gossip site Gawker started a new era in blogging.

Former *Financial Times* reporter and tech entrepreneur Nick Denton founded the site from his loft in 2002. He'd later say, "Gawker writers, plugged into the journalists' gossip networks, looked for the story behind the story, the version that was shared over a drink but less frequently published."

The vibe was purposefully mean.

Tabloid media always poked at the celebrities they covered, but Gawker made its brand about really going after its subjects. This got the site a lot of clicks from readers who liked seeing people get taken down.

> **QUIZ**
>
> **Which of these niche sites did *not* spawn from New York–centric Gawker?**
>
> **A.** Gizmodo
> **B.** Spinner
> **C.** Wonkette
> **D.** Valleywag
>
> *Quiz Answer:* B.

Gawker sowed the seeds of its own destruction.

In 2007, a Gawker site ran an article headlined, "Peter Thiel is totally gay, people." The billionaire tech entrepreneur and venture capitalist wasn't happy. He'd later fund a lawsuit by pro wrestler Hulk Hogan against Gawker Media for publishing a sex tape in which Hogan appeared. The suit bankrupted Denton's company.

Arianna Huffington took on *Drudge* in 2005.

Huffington started her namesake news site, *The Huffington Post*, to provide a progressive counter to right-leaning news site *The Drudge Report*.

Huffington's first website was Resignation.com.

The site, which attracted and empowered conservatives, called for President Bill Clinton to resign after his sex scandal.

Like *Drudge*, *HuffPost* was a news aggregator.

The company essentially scraped news from other publications, reshaped it, and republished it without doing (or paying for) any of the journalistic work.

HuffPost was known for not paying their writers.

The site had tons of content, much of it generated by highly productive bloggers. Except for a few big names, almost everybody who wrote for them was unpaid.

Within about a year, the site was getting over 2 million visitors a month.

HuffPost quickly broke away from politics to cover celebrity gossip, health and wellness, and culture—essentially, anything people would click on. By 2008, it was outpacing traffic for the *Los Angeles Times* and the *Wall Street Journal*.

A *Huffington Post* cofounder started *BuzzFeed* in 2006.

About a year after cofounding *HuffPost*, MIT grad and trained trend hunter Jonah Peretti put his knowledge of virality to work to cocreate another Internet giant.

The site started as just another click-baiting aggregator.

Then, Peretti hired writers and started generating more original content, including actual reporting from brash young writers already steeped in Internet lore.

They didn't create the listicle, but they perfected it.

BuzzFeed became so well known for their viral listicles filled with GIFs and goofy photos attuned to each item that one of their writers actually wrote an *Onion*-like satire on the form called "20 Things Only Heirs to the Martian Throne Will Understand."

Their target market was anyone who was bored at work.

A big part of *BuzzFeed*'s success seemed to hinge on readers who didn't have enough to do at work and wanted to kill time online. (There have been worse business models.)

BuzzFeed's former editor in chief gave away the formula.

Ben Smith said a big part of the company's approach to staying relevant in a newly social world is "scoops and exclusives and original content, and it's also about cute kittens in an entertaining cultural context."

Netflix tried to sell the business to Blockbuster in 2000.

Mailing DVDs was a hit-and-miss proposition in the first few years. In 2000, Netflix was so desperate for money that they offered to sell half of the company to Blockbuster (the reigning champion of home movie-watching) for just $50 million. Blockbuster said no.

Walmart tried to poach Netflix's business in 2002.

Once Netflix proved how profitable their business model could be, Walmart copied it, starting their own DVD subscription service. The big-box store conceded to Netflix three years later.

QUIZ

In what year did Netflix get into the streaming game?

A. 2002
B. 2003
C. 2006
D. 2007

Quiz Answer: D.

By 2006, people couldn't imagine their lives without Netflix.

They had 6.3 million subscribers and $1 billion annual revenue, and they had shipped over 1 billion DVDs.

Blockbuster came to regret their choices by the end of the aughts.

The video chain had more than 9,000 stores at its height in 2004. By 2010, the popularity of streaming had led Blockbuster to bankruptcy.

PayPal employees created YouTube as a video-dating service.

Chad Hurley, Steve Chen, and Jawed Karim registered the site YouTube.com on Valentine's Day in 2005 with the slogan "Tune In, Hook Up."

The dating site lasted one week.

Despite offering people $20 on Craigslist to upload their dating videos, YouTube didn't have any takers. The founders immediately pivoted to letting users upload and share any kind of video.

QUIZ

Which popular site helped YouTube find its footing?

A. Gawker

B. Twitter

C. MySpace

D. I Can Has Cheezburger

Quiz Answer: C.

YouTube got sued for copyright infringement. A lot.

Users started posting copyrighted material more rapidly than the site's small staff could pull it down, but they kept trying. That concerted effort to uphold the law is why entertainment conglomerate Viacom, which owned channels like MTV and Comedy Central, ultimately lost their $1 billion lawsuit in 2007.

YouTube started harnessing copyrighted content for profit.

Multiple people uploaded *Saturday Night Live*'s "Lazy Sunday" sketch, but NBC didn't worry about it too much. The video was driving people to watch the show. Spotting an opportunity, YouTube started signing deals with companies to let the site run clips of their material.

Google acquired YouTube for $1.65 billion in 2006.

The search giant already had its own service, Google Video, which was popular for its educational fare. But it couldn't compete with YouTube, whose users were watching about 100 million videos daily.

That same year, Amazon got into the game.

Leaving no stone unturned in its pell-mell drive to business domination, Amazon added its VOD (video on demand) service, Amazon Prime Video, in 2006.

Apple's iTunes Store quietly changed how we watch TV in 2005.

Apple added TV shows to the iTunes Store, allowing users to legally purchase and download episodes of hit shows for $1.99 each and proving that people would pay for digital distribution.

Joost was the future—until it wasn't.

Launched in 2007 by the founders of Skype, Joost was an ambitious peer-to-peer video-streaming platform backed by big names like CBS and Viacom. It died a quiet death thanks to YouTube and Hulu.

Hulu represented the networks in 2008.

The ad-supported streaming service was born out of a partnership between NBC and Fox, which were looking for a way to make their shows available online while retaining control.

"THIS BEAT IS AUTOMATIC,
SUPERSONIC, HYPNOTIC,
FUNKY FRESH.

WORK MY BODY, SO MELODIC,
THIS BEAT ROLLS RIGHT
THROUGH MY CHEST."

—"1, 2 Step," Ciara featuring Missy Elliott

BEATS, RHYMES, and RIFFS

Music That Ruled the 2000s

Napster helped 60 million users pirate music.

The file-sharing site's reign was brief (1999 to 2001). But in those two years, it forever changed the way people accessed music.

The aughts saw music revenue drop by more than half.

The record industry generated $14.6 billion in sales revenue in 1999. By 2009, that number dropped down to $6.3 billion as digital downloads and streaming services steadily rose in popularity over the decade.

QUIZ

Which musical group got into a trademark battle with Apple?

A. The Beatles

B. Sublime

C. U2

D. Black Eyed Peas

Quiz Answer: A.

The iTunes Store launched in 2003.

As the first broadly accessible and easy-to-use digital music service, Apple finally gave people a way to buy and store music on their computers without breaking the law.

Apple CEO Steve Jobs was the genius behind being able to purchase a single song.

He priced them at 99 cents each and convinced most major music companies to sign up.

The iTunes Store started with 200,000 songs.

They included exclusives from artists like Bob Dylan, Eminem, and Sheryl Crow. Customers bought a million songs in the first week. That number reached 3 *billion* in 2007.

The iPod put "1,000 songs in your pocket" in November 2001.

Of all the decade's big Apple tech reveals, the launch of the iPod (with its killer tagline) was one of the few that really lived up to the hype.

By 2004, Apple had sold over 2 million units.

The iTunes Store helped the iPod's popularity by enabling users to upload music directly from iTunes to their iPods.

Then came the Mini, the Shuffle, and the Nano.

Released in 2004 and 2005, these iPod variations brought color, convenience, and cost-effectiveness to the line.

The iPod's storage jumped from 5 GB to 160 GB by 2007.

It needed the extra space to accommodate its handy new touch screen.

The ads were unforgettable.

Apple's "Silhouette" ads in 2003 were intensely cool, featuring black silhouettes of people dancing in front of solid-colored backgrounds. Later waves featured bands like Jet and U2.

Microsoft's Zune was the better machine but failed anyway.

Experts believed that Microsoft's MP3 player, launched in 2006, was the better-designed piece of hardware, with a far more user-friendly interface. Unfortunately, few people bought one.

The MTV Video Music Awards persisted longer than music videos did.

Even though MTV and VH1 were largely done with showing music videos by the early 2000s, the annual VMAs continued to bring together big-name artists and generate buzz.

A kiss at the 2003 VMAs turned heads and made headlines.

Madonna kissed both Britney Spears and Christina Aguilera, though most people watching on TV never saw the Aguilera kiss. The show's director cut away from it to show Spears' ex-boyfriend Justin Timberlake.

Panic! at the Disco brought circus goth to prime time in 2006.

Their performance of "I Write Sins Not Tragedies" turned the VMAs into a Tim Burton fever dream—top hats, contortionists, and all. They ended up winning Video of the Year, even though MTV barely played their video.

Beyoncé gave a jaw-dropping performance that same year.

The singer literally dropped from the ceiling to perform "Ring the Alarm" while flanked by lights, sirens, and backup dancers in trench coats.

Lady Gaga made her VMA debut in 2009.

She performed "Paparazzi" in full theatrical mode: wide eyes, white lace, and a staged breakdown that left her bloodied and sprawled on stage. It was weird, campy, and unforgettable.

Beyoncé set a music-industry record in 2003.

She became the first female artist to have the number-one single ("Crazy in Love") and album (*Dangerously in Love*) at the same time in both the United States and the United Kingdom.

Queen Bey made her acting debut in 2002.

The makers of *Austin Powers in Goldmember* (2002) cast Beyoncé as FBI agent/nightclub chanteuse Foxxy Cleopatra. The role launched her somewhat short acting career, which peaked with a Golden Globe nomination for 2006's musical *Dreamgirls*.

QUIZ

What was Beyoncé's first post–Destiny's Child solo album called?

A. *Lemonade*

B. *Beyoncé*

C. *I Am... Sasha Fierce*

D. *Dangerously in Love*

Quiz Answer: D.

Beyoncé's 2008 wedding to Jay-Z included 40 guests, 70,000 orchids, and no media.

At a time when many celebrities were setting up their weddings like big-budget PR productions, theirs was a study in privacy. Of course, that doesn't mean it was low-key; their florist flew in those 70,000 orchids from Thailand to adorn Jay-Z's lavish Tribeca penthouse.

I Am... Sasha Fierce earned Beyoncé six Grammies.

The 2008 album also included the runaway hit "Single Ladies." Its iconic black-and-white video features Beyoncé and two ballerinas performing a variation on a Bob Fosse routine from *The Ed Sullivan Show* in 1969.

Jay-Z's big 2003 retirement turned into more of a sabbatical.

Three years after his retirement blowout and concert at Madison Square Garden, footage from which was made into the 2004 documentary *Fade to Black*, he dropped a new album: *Kingdom Come*.

The Black Album would have capped off an amazing career perfectly.

Ranging from autobiographical reflections ("December 4") to full-on bangers ("99 Problems"), it became a massive hit, was nominated for a Grammy, and boosted the career of collaborator John Legend.

QUIZ

Which megastar secretly sang on a remix of Jay-Z's hit single "Girls, Girls, Girls"?

A. Paul McCartney
B. Michael Jackson
C. Beyoncé
D. Busta Rhymes

Quiz Answer: B.

It accidentally kicked off his role as a fashion influencer.

The Black Album's "What More Can I Say" saw Jay-Z declare, "I don't wear jerseys, I'm 30-plus" while noting he was more into "a crisp pair of jeans" and "button-ups." That's exactly what he wore to *GQ*'s Men of the Year Awards in 2003, and other rappers followed suit.

We have Jay-Z to thank for kick-starting another music-industry mogul's career.

As president and CEO of Def Jam Records in 2005, Jay-Z signed then sixteen-year-old Rihanna after hearing just one song. She received her first Grammy Award three years later.

Danger Mouse made the decade's biggest mash-up.

His experimental 2004 *The Grey Album* wove parts of The Beatles' *The White Album* throughout Jay-Z's *The Black Album*, creating an unexpectedly intoxicating blend.

It had the artists' blessing.

Jay-Z, who released a cappella versions of his songs specifically so others could remix them, called the mash-up a "genius idea," while Paul McCartney saw it as a tribute and called it a full-circle moment.

The Beatles' copyright holder, EMI, wasn't a fan.

They called for retailers to cease distribution, resulting in a massive "Grey Tuesday" protest orchestrated by activist group Downhill Battle and more than 100,000 downloads of the album.

Danger Mouse was flummoxed by the uproar.

Brian Joseph Burton (aka Danger Mouse) said he'd only intended to create an art project, not to break any copyright laws. Luckily, none of the protesters who bought the album actually faced legal repercussions.

Jay-Z found new inspiration for a mash-up in metal.

After *The Grey Album*, Jay-Z decided to try a collaboration with nu-metal group Linkin Park. Their collaboration, *Collision Course*, came out in 2004 and went double platinum.

The Strokes brought back garage rock in 2001.

The 1960s West Coast sound characterized by bands like the Sonics gave way to punk in the 1970s before boomeranging back in the 2000s.

The Yeah Yeah Yeahs kept the garage rock coming.

Another loud-rocking New York indie band who hit the ground running, this trio had a critical darling of a debut (2003's *Fever to Tell*) and a singer (Karen O) whose yelping vocals and idiosyncratic fashion sense captured attention.

Even the Brits got in on it.

The Arctic Monkeys' *Whatever People Say I Am, That's What I'm Not* introduced a denser, riffier style of garage rock that expanded the mini-genre from its back-to-roots origins.

The White Stripes had the most longevity.

This raw two-person blues-rock unit (Jack White as guitarist and vocalist with his then-wife Meg White pounding away on drums) won two Grammys for Best Alternative Music Album: *Elephant* (2004) and *Get Behind Me Satan* (2006).

QUIZ

Which album landed the Strokes in the spotlight?

A. *This Is It*

B. *The New Abnormal*

C. *Room on Fire*

D. *Comedown Machine*

Quiz Answer: A.

The Stripes' "Seven Nation Army" became a global stadium chant.

In 2003, Club Brugge fans spontaneously began chanting the riff while pregaming before a match against A. C. Milan. The chant caught on across Europe and was famously used by Italian fans when Italy won the 2006 World Cup.

The song's name comes from a childhood misunderstanding.

Singer/songwriter Jack White misheard "Salvation Army" as "Seven Nation Army" when he was a child.

Gary Glitter's downfall forced a shift in stadium anthems.

For decades, Glitter's "Rock and Roll Part 2" (the "Hey" song) was a stadium mainstay. After his 2006 conviction for child sex offenses, many American teams began phasing the song out and seeking new anthems.

Arena playlists became hyper-local in the 2000s.

Many teams began incorporating local artists and regional favorites into their game-day soundtracks. Jay-Z became a Brooklyn Nets staple, Nirvana riffs rang through Seattle stadiums, and Dropkick Murphys became anthemic in Boston arenas.

Hip-hop went from the parking lot to the arena playlist.

In the 2000s, hip-hop became a fixture inside arenas. Songs like DMX's "Party Up (Up in Here)" and Kanye West's "Stronger" were crowd-pumping staples.

Nelly was one of the biggest breakout rappers of the early 2000s.

His debut album *Country Grammar* (2000) peaked at No. 1 on the Billboard 200. It's still one of the best-selling rap albums of all time, with more than 10 million copies sold in the United States.

The St. Louis, Missouri, native brought Midwestern hip-hop into the mainstream.

Nelly was part of a new wave of artists coming from outside New York and California that included Master P (New Orleans, Louisiana), OutKast and Ludacris (Atlanta, Georgia), and Scarface (Houston, Texas).

You couldn't escape his singles in the 2000s.

Nelly's infectious pop-rap single "Ride Wit Me" was everywhere for much of 2000. "Hot in Herre" from *Nellyville* (2002) went even bigger.

Nelly brought pimp juice to the masses.

"Pimp Juice" was a Nelly single from 2003 that had a brief run in the clubs and on the radio. You could even find it in a can: a beverage of the same name, co-owned by the rapper, was branded as "Hip-Hop's #1 Energy Drink."

He's one of few artists who have performed at multiple Super Bowls.

Nelly was part of the halftime shows in both 2001 and 2004.

Mixtapes changed the game for hip-hop artists in the 2000s.

What started out as freely shared DJ-mixed collections of artists freestyling over existing beats became a conduit for delivering new music under the radar to build momentum without having to go through a record label.

50 Cent built his career on mixtapes.

After barely surviving being shot nine times and subsequently being dropped by Columbia Records, 50 Cent went the nontraditional route. He used street bootleggers to sell mixtapes like *50 Cent Is the Future* and *Guess Who's Back?*, which caught the attention of Eminem in 2002.

QUIZ

Which rapper has 50 Cent *not* had a beef with?

A. Cam'ron

B. Diddy

C. Drake

D. Lil Wayne

Quiz Answer: C.

Eminem's label, Shady Records, gave the rapper a $1 million record deal.

The *8 Mile* artist invited 50 Cent to Los Angeles and introduced him to producer Dr. Dre.

50 Cent's 2003 album *Get Rich or Die Tryin'* went multiplatinum.

It delivered hit singles like "In da Club," which became an anthem for the decade. Critics liked it. Then he starred in a movie of the same name two years later. Critics did *not* like that.

Eminem was the best-selling US artist of the decade.

The Detroit rapper made noise in 1999 with *The Slim Shady EP* when "My Name Is" went wide on MTV. But *The Marshall Mathers LP* made him a music icon.

The newly minted movie star slept through his Oscar win.

When "Lose Yourself" from Eminem's autobiographical 2002 movie *8 Mile* won the Oscar for Best Original Song, he was at home, asleep, because he didn't think he had a shot at the award.

He turned diss tracks into an art form.

There are entire fan-curated spreadsheets cataloging the people Eminem has name-dropped, mocked, or torched in his songs, including Moby, Britney Spears, Christina Aguilera, Carson Daly, and his own mom.

The Secret Service investigated Eminem in 2003.

The lyrics, "I don't rap for dead presidents / I'd rather see the president dead" in a bootleg recording of "We as Americans" troubled President George W. Bush's security detail.

QUIZ

Which Gen Z slang word came from an Eminem song of the same name?

A. Vibe

B. Simp

C. Flex

D. Stan

Quiz Answer: D.

Coldplay made their US television debut with "Yellow" in 2001 on *Late Night with Conan O'Brien*.

The hit single from the British band's debut album *Parachutes* made them one of the world's most popular bands.

Lead singer Chris Martin got the idea for "Yellow" from the phone book.

He was looking for inspiration in the chorus when he saw the Yellow Pages sitting nearby.

Parachutes won Best Alternative Album at the 2002 Grammys.

The album went platinum many times over, as did follow-up albums *A Rush of Blood to the Head* (2002), *X&Y* (2005), and *Viva la Vida* (2008). *A Rush of Blood to the Head* won the Best Alt Album Grammy in 2003.

Hip-hop took an interest in the band.

Martin collaborated with both Jay-Z and Kanye West, while Coldplay was sampled by Swizz Beatz and covered by Frank Ocean.

Martin married fellow 2000s icon Gwyneth Paltrow in 2003.

They welcomed their daughter, Apple, in 2004, and their son, Moses, in 2006. ("Apple" topped many a list of slightly odd celebrity baby names during the decade.)

Chris Martin and lead guitarist Jonny Buckland have a cameo in *Shaun of the Dead* (2004).

They played "zombie sympathizers."

Justin Timberlake went solo at the 2002 MTV Video Music Awards.

Ironically, his *NSYNC bandmates introduced the performance that helped him break out of the band (which had been suffering from burnout and considering a hiatus).

His first album, *Justified* (2002), sold more than 7 million copies.

Packed with eminently danceable singles, it delivered Timberlake two Grammys, not to mention a nomination for Favorite Male Singer from the Nickelodeon Kids' Choice Awards.

Timberlake created an iconic *Saturday Night Live* musical sketch in 2006.

Showing off his comedy chops for the first time while hosting *SNL*, the singer costarred with Andy Samberg in "D*** in a Box."

He broke into the (animated) movie business in 2007.

He voiced Artie in *Shrek the Third*.

QUIZ

Which 2000s starlet did Timberlake *not* date?

A. Cameron Diaz

B. Mila Kunis

C. Fergie

D. Alyssa Milano

Quiz Answer: B.

In 2010, the singer-turned-actor played the cofounder of Napster.

Timberlake played Sean Parker, cofounder of Napster—the music service not exactly beloved by musicians—in David Fincher's Facebook movie *The Social Network*.

Justin Bieber made his way to stardom using YouTube.

Music exec Scooter Braun saw one of the singer's videos and was blown away by him. In 2008, Braun flew thirteen-year-old Bieber and his mother to Atlanta to sign him.

Bieber taught himself how to play multiple instruments.

In addition to having a voice that launched a thousand teenage screams, the multitalented musician could also play guitar, piano, drums, and trumpet.

Justin Timberlake lost out to Usher on signing the tween sensation.

Braun first reached out to Timberlake to back Bieber, but when Usher caught wind of the Canadian music prodigy, he made the bigger play to sign him.

Bieber's music caught on fast.

Singles like "One Less Lonely Girl" electrified the tween market in 2009 and secured him a Grammy nomination for Best New Artist in 2011.

"Baby" was one of the most disliked videos on YouTube.

Released in 2010, Bieber's breakout hit "Baby" exploded online—but it also drew tons of hate-clicks. It held the record as the most-disliked video on YouTube until 2018.

MySpace helped emo ("emotional hardcore") music flourish.

Bands like Fall Out Boy and Panic! at the Disco were fixtures of the site, which allowed users to set their own pages to music.

Pete Wentz became the accidental poster boy for emo.

Fall Out Boy's bassist was a fixture on magazine covers in the early 2000s, with his long black bangs, "guyliner," and brooding stare.

My Chemical Romance rejected the "emo" label.

Despite being synonymous with the emo era, lead vocalist Gerard Way was quoted as saying the style is "garbage" (among other, saltier takes).

Jimmy Eat World redefined emo.

Their 2001 single "The Middle" made them the new face of the genre even though the band hadn't yet embraced the label. (Bassist Rick Burch called it "limiting.")

In 2008, *Daily Mail* called emo a "sinister cult."

The article said listening to emo would lead a child to rebellion, self-harm, and suicide. Instead, it led to teenage fans protesting outside of the paper's headquarters.

Green Day helped pop punk break out.

By the 2000s, a squad of bands who emulated the hook-heavy, sing-along Green Day style started amassing fans and filling arenas.

Blink-182 and Fall Out Boy took the baton and ran with it.

Adolescent humor, catchy songs, and crashing guitars gained these bands a lot of radio play.

Hot Topic carried the best pop-punk gear.

The mall chain helped emo and pop-punk teens find the right black T-shirts, makeup, and bondage pants (the ones with all the chains and straps hanging off).

Vans became part of the dress code.

The iconic skater shoe company's annual summer *Warped* tour brought punk and pop-punk bands like Bad Religion and Blink-182 together with fans from 1995 to 2019, then reemerged in 2025.

QUIZ

Which celeb made a cameo in Fall Out Boy's "Thnks fr th Mmrs" (2007)?

A. Lindsay Lohan

B. Kim Kardashian

C. Matt Damon

D. Paris Hilton

Quiz Answer: B.

Stacy's mom had it goin' on.

Although power-pop band Fountains of Wayne had been around since 1995, it wasn't until 2003 that most people heard of them. That year, their third album, *Welcome Interstate Managers*, delivered the single "Stacy's Mom," an up-tempo goof that went gold.

Afroman earned a Grammy nod by appealing to pot smokers.

In addition to the nomination, rapper Afroman's 2000 "Because I Got High" earned prominent placement in the 2001 movie *Jay and Silent Bob Strike Back*.

The Baha Men let the dogs out in 2000.

The novelty number "Who Let the Dogs Out" by the Bahamian one-hit wonders never really left us, perhaps because its central question remained unanswered.

Blu Cantrell's relationship advice hit No. 2 on *Billboard*'s Hot 100.

The onetime backup vocalist was instantly everywhere when her first single "Hit 'Em Up Style (Oops!)" came out in 2001 and told jilted listeners to "get your hands on his cash and spend it to the last dime."

QUIZ

Which of these one-hit wonders hit it big in the 2000s?

A. Right Said Fred
B. Gerardo
C. Chumbawamba
D. Trapt

Quiz Answer: D.

The Pussycat Dolls started out as a burlesque group.

They regularly performed at Johnny Depp's Los Angeles club the Viper Room into the early 2000s.

Celebrities flocked to their ranks.

The group attracted big-name guest burlesquers like Christina Applegate, Charlize Theron, Christina Aguilera, Gwen Stefani, P!nk, and Scarlett Johansson.

The Dolls had a cameo in 2003's *Charlie's Angels: Full Throttle.*

The Pussycat Dolls helped the Angels (played by Drew Barrymore, Lisa Liu, and Cameron Diaz) distract the bad guy with a dance while stealing his keys.

Producer Jimmy Iovine of Interscope Geffen A&M Records saw their musical potential.

He had the idea to parlay the Pussycat Dolls into a pop group based on the burlesque brand. Instead of using celebrity dancers, they brought in singers.

The Dolls' first album, *PCD* (2005), was a massive hit.

The group even toured with the Black Eyed Peas. But by 2010, the Dolls had gone their separate ways due to bad blood.

The Pussycat Dolls inspired 2010's star-studded *Burlesque.*

The movie featured Cher, Christina Aguilera, Stanley Tucci, Alan Cumming, Kristen Bell, Julianne Hough, and Peter Gallagher.

Long-established artists headlined the biggest tours of the decade.

Canadian balladeer Celine Dion made the list of the top ten highest-grossing tours, right above AC/DC and a few rungs below The Police and Madonna.

Prince barred his bandmates from wearing the color purple from his 2004 tour.

The singer wanted his signature color to himself during his *Musicology* tour.

Cher's "farewell tour" lasted three years.

The subtitle of the singer's 2002 *Living Proof* tour was definitive: *The Farewell Tour*. It was technically correct, because the last show of that tour (in 2005) was, in fact, her last live show.

That tour earned Cher a Guinness World Record.

It was the highest-grossing tour by a single female artist at the time, earning more than $200 million. (No wonder she didn't stop performing.)

The Rolling Stones had the highest-grossing tour of the aughts.

Their *A Bigger Bang* tour (2005–2007) grossed over $558 million.

QUIZ

Which artist broke Cher's record before the end of the decade?

A. Madonna
B. Beyoncé
C. Tina Turner
D. Celine Dion

Quiz Answer: A.

A mathematician who used to work for Exxon invented Auto-Tune.

Dr. Andy Hildebrand's company released the software in 1997 to subtly (or not so subtly) correct imperfections in a singer's pitch.

Cher set it up to be a defining feature of the 2000s.

Her 1998 single "Believe" was the first big hit to use the software intentionally.

T-Pain made it his artistic identity.

In the mid-2000s, he actually stopped rapping altogether and shifted to singing that was heavily juiced by Auto-Tune for his 2005 album *Rappa Ternt Sanga*.

Yeezy followed suit after meeting up with T-Pain in Hawaii.

Kanye West's *very* Auto-Tuned 2009 album *808 & Heartbreak* was a break from his earlier work and a favorite of critics.

Jay-Z tried to kill Auto-Tune and failed.

His 2009 single "D.O.A. (Death of Auto-Tune)" called for rappers to stop leaning on the effect. The song made headlines, but artists continued using Auto-Tune well into the 2010s and beyond.

Death Cab for Cutie publicly protested the software's ubiquity.

They wore blue ribbons to the 2009 Grammy Awards to signal their disdain. (It was a mild protest—very on-brand.)

Christina Aguilera proved she could hold her own with the "Lady Marmalade" collab.

The former Mouseketeer didn't shy away from multi-octave acrobatics, which helped her earn a 2002 Grammy Award for Best Collaboration alongside P!nk, Mýa, and Lil' Kim.

Aguilera cowrote Kelly Clarkson's breakout hit.

Also a talented writer, Aguilera worked on 2003's "Miss Independent."

Her 2002 music video for "Dirrty" faced backlash for being too sexy.

Other artists said it went too far, and her record label in Thailand would not show the video because it featured Thai-language posters advertising "sex tourism" and "underage girls." Still, the song climbed every chart.

QUIZ

What was Rihanna's breakout hit?

A. "Unfaithful"

B. "SOS"

C. "Pon de Replay"

D. "Lucky"

Quiz Answer: C.

Rihanna's body-baring hit "Umbrella" (2007) almost belonged to Britney Spears.

The pop star passed on it. So did Mary J. Blige. It was their loss because that single, released as part of the album *Good Girl Gone Bad*, cemented Rihanna in the decade's music canon.

The SOS singer had a cameo as herself in 2006's *Bring It On: All or Nothing*.

The film starred Hayden Panettiere and Solange Knowles as rival cheerleaders.

A Lebanese-Colombian belly dancer proved a surprise success among pop singers.

Shakira's first English-language album, *Laundry Service* (2001), with its up-tempo hit "Whenever, Wherever," sold about 13 million copies. The video highlighted her hip-shaking talents.

She wrote, composed, translated, and produced "Whenever, Wherever" herself.

Music legend Gloria Estefan helped her finalize it for the American market.

A record exec told P!nk to "go solo or go home."

L. A. Reid gave her the ultimatum at a Christmas party about the R&B group, Choice, she formed with friends at the age of fifteen. She put out her first solo album, *Can't Take Me Home*, in 2000. It went double platinum.

She used *Missundaztood* (2001) to break out of the pop-star mold.

Billboard named it one of its top 200 albums.

It took Katy Perry six years to break through.

Born Katheryn Hudson, the singer made an unsuccessful gospel album and had been dropped by Columbia Records before releasing "I Kissed a Girl" with Capitol Records in 2008.

Teenage Dream made *Billboard* history.

In 2010, Perry became the first woman—and second artist ever, after Michael Jackson—to score five number-one singles from the same album.

Lady Gaga's debut album generated six singles.

2008's *The Fame* included "Just Dance," "Poker Face," "Love Game," and "Paparazzi," as well as "Eh, Eh (Nothing Else I Can Say)" (limited) and "Beautiful, Dirty, Rich" (promotional).

The deluxe edition was a monster hit.

Interscope Records planned to release *The Fame Monster* as a deluxe edition of the album, but it took on its own life when Gaga added eight conceptually different songs. Those included the iconic lead single "Bad Romance."

The Fame earned Lady Gaga five Grammy nominations.

Not only did she win two awards, but she also performed for the event: a number with a big quasi-Frankenstein stage set called "The Fame Factory" that included Gaga and Elton John playing opposite ends of the same piano.

Lady Gaga's looks took nearly as much work as her music.

The outfits she wore consistently made headlines, from her corseted dress made of hair for the 2009 MuchMusic Video Awards to her bubble dress at the House of Blues and more.

QUIZ

Which was *not* part of a costume Gaga wore?

A. Fire bra

B. Live butterflies

C. Bleeding bodysuit

D. Raw meat

Quiz Answer: B.

Amy Winehouse brought smoky jazz singing back to pop music in 2003.

The North London original was just twenty when she cut her debut, a jazz album called *Frank*. Though it wasn't released in the United States, it built anticipation for her next project.

Back to Black earned her five Grammys.

This 2006 album was a highly unlikely success, combining Winehouse's rich girl-group vocals with raw confessional lyrics and the gritty early Motown sound of her backup band, the Dap-Kings.

Many of her songs were autobiographical.

Much of *Back to Black* was about Winehouse's personal life, including her struggles with addiction ("Rehab") and tumultuous relationship with her partner, Blake Fielder-Civil.

As the song goes, "they" really did try to make Winehouse go to rehab.

Manager Nick Shymansky encouraged her to enter rehab in 2005. She finally went in 2008 but died of alcohol poisoning in 2011.

Without Amy, there may not have been an Adele.

The spectacular success of *Back to Black* helped inspire what was referred to later as the "soul revival," spurring interest in the Dap-Kings and paving the way for Adele, another throwback singer who would break through with 2011's *21*.

Like *The Office, American Idol* got its start in the United Kingdom.

Pop Idol was a huge UK hit after its first season in 2001, so producer Simon Fuller decided to try the same thing across the pond.

Simon Cowell came along for the ride.

He was originally a judge on *Pop Idol.*

The other judges balanced Cowell's cutting (and sometimes cruel) opinions.

Singer and choreographer Paula Abdul had a perennially hopeful outlook, while producer Randy Jackson gave the panel its ballast between the fire-and-ice team on either side of him.

Abdul quit eight times on her first day.

She explained to *Entertainment Weekly* that she "felt terrible" for many of the auditioners.

Like *Pop Idol, American Idol* had two hosts.

Comedian Brian Dunkleman joined Ryan Seacrest on the stage for the first season. Dunkelman bowed out, but Seacrest went on to become a Hollywood powerhouse and one of the producers responsible for introducing the Kardashians to the masses.

QUIZ

Which *Idol* judge said signing on was the "worst decision"?

A. Jennifer Lopez
B. Steven Tyler
C. Ellen DeGeneres
D. Mariah Carey

Quiz Answer: C.

Voters got it right the first time with Kelly Clarkson.

The season-one winner would go on to achieve massive success in the music industry, with countless awards under her belt and her own talk show.

Carrie Underwood veered away from her roots to please Simon Cowell.

After hearing that the judge wasn't a fan of country music, the singer chose "I Can't Make You Love Me."

More than 38 million people watched Ruben Studdard beat out Clay Aiken.

The season-two singers remained close, though, and both went on to achieve platinum albums.

Being outed on *Idol* led Adam Lambert to become an outspoken advocate.

In addition to releasing hit singles like "Whataya Want from Me" and touring with Queen, the season-eight runner-up has dedicated himself to championing LGBTQ+ issues.

Not winning season five launched Katharine McPhee's career.

The runner-up went on to star in the NBC musical drama *Smash* and CBS hit *Scorpion* as well as perform on Broadway.

A number of now-famous singers didn't make it past *Idol* auditions.

Producers rejected "Bubbly" singer Colbie Caillat, Lady A's Hillary Scott, and *Glee*'s Naya Rivera and Amber Riley.

Carrie Underwood was the first country artist to debut at No. 1 on the *Billboard* Hot 100.

The 2025 single "Inside Your Heaven" proved that the season-four *Idol* winner really had what it took to be a star.

"Before He Cheats" helped country music cross over.

Underwood's 2005 hit topped *Billboard*'s Hot Country Songs for five weeks and reached top ten on the *Billboard* Mainstream Top 40 and Adult Contemporary charts.

Pop singer Jessica Simpson gave country music a shot in 2008.

Her album *Do You Know* debuted at No. 1 on *Billboard* Country Albums and No. 4 on *Billboard* 200 but didn't have much success with critics or fans.

Toby Keith was pulled from an ABC Fourth of July special for being a bit too patriotic.

His 2002 track "Courtesy of the Red, White, and Blue (The Angry American)"—a musical reaction to the 9/11 terror attacks—threatened to "put a boot in your ass."

The Chicks (then Dixie Chicks) were canceled by conservatives.

In 2003, lead singer Natalie Maines said she was "ashamed" President George W. Bush was from Texas. Their sales and bookings tanked overnight, but they came back strong in 2006 with their Grammy-winning response, "Not Ready to Make Nice."

Taylor Swift did some modeling before her recording career took off.

Abercrombie & Fitch featured the fourteen-year-old, who had recently signed with record label RCA, in a 2003 ad of "rising stars." (She wore a classic white tee and flare jeans.)

She released her self-titled debut country album in 2006.

Including songs like "Tim McGraw" and "Teardrops on My Guitar," it was the longest-charting album of the decade on the *Billboard* 200, with 157 weeks on the chart.

Swift skipped her senior prom to attend the 2008 Grammy Awards.

The Best New Artist nominee told reporters she was excited to see Foo Fighters, Feist, and Kanye West.

West famously dampened the singer's excitement at the 2009 VMAs.

Swift had just been given the award for Best Female Video for "You Belong with Me" when West darted on stage, took the microphone, and declared that Beyoncé's video for "Single Ladies (Put a Ring on It)" should have won.

QUIZ

What did President Obama call Kanye West for disrupting Taylor Swift's win?

A. Jackass

B. Genius

C. Idiot

D. Right

Quiz Answer: A.

President Obama hosted a poetry jam in 2009.

Def Poetry Jam was canceled in 2007, but Obama decided to bring it back for an event called An Evening of Poetry, Music, and Spoken Word (also known as the "White House Poetry Jam").

The evening featured some of the most talented artists in the country.

James Earl Jones delivered an *Othello* soliloquy, jazz musician Esperanza Spalding covered Lauryn Hill's "Tell Him," and multiple spoken-word artists spoke their words.

The president got the first peek at what would become *Hamilton*.

Lin-Manuel Miranda closed the evening by performing "Alexander Hamilton," which would remain largely unchanged as the first number in the 2015 musical.

Miranda based *Hamilton* on Ron Chernow's 2005 biography of the founding father.

He took the book on vacation with him for some light reading between Broadway and Off-Broadway runs of his first musical, *In the Heights*.

The young songwriter said Alexander Hamilton "embodies hip-hop."

When introducing the rap, Miranda said, "I'm actually working on a hip-hop concept album about the life of someone I think embodies hip-hop: Treasury Secretary Alexander Hamilton. You laugh! But it's true."

Mamma Mia! brought the music of ABBA to Broadway in 2001.

It started a trend of "jukebox musicals," in which a story is spun at often absurd lengths to accommodate the inclusion of preexisting music (usually by one artist whose producers or estate are looking to cash in).

The show played for 14 years and over 5,000 performances on Broadway.

Suddenly, ABBA was everywhere again.

Jersey Boys followed suit in 2005 and won four Tonys.

Less story-driven than *Mamma Mia!*, *Jersey Boys* was more of a concert film that ran one Four Seasons song after another.

Movin' Out was a jukebox musical with almost no speaking.

The 2002 show used Billy Joel songs to tell a coming-of-age story about Vietnam-era teens, but it had zero dialogue. Instead, it relied on choreography by Twyla Tharp to express every twist of the plot.

QUIZ

Which of these jukebox musicals was *not* a flop?

A. *Lennon*

B. *Good Vibrations*

C. *All Shook Up*

D. *Rock of Ages*

Quiz Answer: D.

Stephen Schwartz got the idea to set *Wicked* to music while on vacation.

The lyricist and composer read Gregory Maguire's novel, which tells the story of L. Frank Baum's *The Wonderful Wizard of Oz* from the point of view of the Wicked Witch, while on holiday in Hawaii and immediately got to work on obtaining the rights.

Wicked got an unexpected boost from Tumblr.

When *Wicked* debuted in 2003, critics were lukewarm, but theater kids were obsessed. Fans flooded early message boards and, later, Tumblr with fan art, fan fiction, and live-bootleg audio trades.

Avenue Q beat *Wicked* for Best Musical.

The raunchy puppet musical, featuring songs like "Everyone's a Little Bit Racist" and "The Internet Is for Porn," beat out *Wicked* at the 2004 Tony Awards. The show was low-budget and irreverent and ran for six years.

Spring Awakening featured several future *Glee* actors.

The edgy 2006 rock musical (about German teens discovering sex, angst, and repression) didn't just win Tonys; it also helped introduce the world to Lea Michele, Jonathan Groff, and Phoebe Strole.

QUIZ

Which actress originated the role of Elphaba in *Wicked*?

A. Eden Espinosa
B. Idina Menzel
C. Ana Gasteyer
D. Kristin Chenoweth

Quiz Answer: B.

The Producers opened on Broadway in 2001.

Starring Nathan Lane and Matthew Broderick, the musical was an adaptation of Mel Brooks's 1967 cult-classic movie about two producers who scheme to get rich through a loophole by making an intentionally bad stage musical (*Springtime for Hitler*), only to have it somehow succeed.

It was the biggest thing that had hit Broadway in years.

Reviews were rapturous. Audiences couldn't get to it fast enough. Suddenly, people who *never* talked about Broadway shows were desperate to get tickets. It was a bona fide phenomenon.

The Producers popularized the idea of "premium seating."

Because demand was so high, the show put aside a small number of incredibly expensive tickets for each show. At the time, the idea of paying $480 for a Broadway show was seen as scandalous—then it became depressingly common.

Its numbers were staggering.

The Producers' original Broadway production ran until 2007, with 2,502 performances and winning twelve Tony Awards. When Lane and Broderick returned for a limited run between December 2003 and April 2004, the show broke a revenue record, earning more than $1.6 million gross in just a single week with eight performances.

"I FEEL LIKE
I JUST FOUND OUT
MY FAVORITE LOVE SONG
WAS WRITTEN ABOUT
A SANDWICH."

—Jane, 27 Dresses

CTRL + ALT + ENTER-TAINMENT

TV, Blockbusters, and Sporting Events

Friends was still going strong (and making bank) into the 2000s.

By the final season (2003–2004), each of the six stars was making a cool $1 million per episode—a TV record at the time. The season cost NBC about $10 million per episode to produce.

About one in six Americans watched the last *Friends* episode.

The *Friends* finale, broadcast on May 6, 2004, had an audience of 52.5 million people.

QUIZ

Monica and Chandler have twins in the *Friends* finale. What were their names?

A. Erica and Jack
B. Phoebe and Joey
C. Emma and Gunther
D. Leslie and Frank

Quiz Answer: A.

Jennifer Aniston almost didn't come back for season ten.

Aniston was the last to sign on, unsure if she wanted to return at all. For one thing, she'd just done *The Good Girl* and was eyeing a film career. The others agreed to shorten the season to eighteen episodes to keep the cast intact.

About 18.4 million NBC viewers also said goodbye to *Will & Grace*.

By the end in 2006, all four leads—Eric McCormack, Debra Messing, Megan Mullally, and Sean Hayes—had won Emmys for their roles.

***How I Met Your Mother* (2005–2014) filled the hole left by *Friends*—and got criticized for it.**

The show poked fun at the comparisons in season two, episode seven ("Swarley"), when Barney says, "Hanging out at a coffee place is not nearly as much fun as hanging out at a bar."

***The Big Bang Theory*'s Jim Parsons auditioned for the role of Barney Stinson.**

Without his Dr. Sheldon Cooper, the science-centric show that ran from 2007 to 2019 might have been wildly different.

The creators of *It's Always Sunny in Philadelphia* (2005) started out making the show themselves.

Rob McElhenney, Glenn Howerton, Charlie Day, and Jordan Reid (the original Dee) wrote, acted, and recorded two episodes that would convince FX to hire them.

Everyone told Danny Devito not to join *Sunny*, despite his interest in the character of Frank.

Everyone except his kids, whose love for the show helped convince him to follow his gut and take the part.

Ron Howard had no intention of narrating *Arrested Development* (2003–2006).

As the cocreator and executive producer of the show, he filled in as narrator for the pilot with every intention of hiring someone else later, but everyone decided he was the perfect fit.

The Office came to America in 2005.

This show was based on Ricky Gervais's British sitcom of the same name, but the BBC version ran for 14 episodes. NBC's version ran for nine seasons and ended with 201 episodes.

It introduced the country to the "mockumentary" sitcom.

Unlike most sitcoms, which had been shot with three cameras and a live studio audience since *I Love Lucy*, *The Office* was styled to look like a documentary, with a shaky handheld feel and characters occasionally playing directly to the camera.

The ratings started off terrible.

At the end of *The Office*'s first season, it ranked 102 out of all 156 broadcast television shows and had lost 57 percent of its original viewers. But it found its groove in season two.

Despite playing the world's worst boss, Steve Carell became a star.

Carell left behind Dunder Mifflin's unctuous, vain, and dopey Michael Scott after season seven to pursue a massively successful film career.

Famous directors flocked to the show.

The Office was seen as so subversively funny that directors like J. J. Abrams (*Star Trek*), Harold Ramis (*Groundhog Day*), and Joss Whedon (*The Avengers*) got in line to shoot episodes.

Parks and Recreation (2009–2015) was supposed to be a spin-off of *The Office.*

NBC wanted to build on the latter's success, but creators Greg Daniels and Michael Schur ultimately decided to tell a new story in the mockumentary style.

Rob Lowe was supposed to be the main character in *The West Wing* (1999–2006).

Between the show pivoting to feature an ensemble cast and some behind-the-scenes drama, Lowe left the show in 2003. (He joined *Parks and Rec* in 2010.)

The final season of *Community* (2009–2015) was shot in a basement beneath *Parks and Rec.*

After *Community* was moved from Paramount to CBS Radford Studios, writers added Greendale's construction to the script to account for the basement pillars popping up in scenes.

QUIZ

On *Scrubs*, which character was originally written as a figment of J. D.'s imagination?

A. Turk

B. The Janitor

C. Dr. Cox

D. Rowdy

Quiz Answer: B.

Community's Donald Glover wrote and acted for *30 Rock* (2006–2013).

In addition to roles as Young P. A., Gay Kid, and Young Tracy Jordan throughout the seasons, Glover was a staff writer and script supervisor for the show from 2006 to 2009.

Tween girls took over Disney Channel in the 2000s.

From *Hannah Montana* and *Lizzie McGuire* to *That's So Raven* and *Wizards of Waverly Place*, the shows helped launch the careers of stars like Miley Cyrus, Emily Osment, Hilary Duff, and Selena Gomez.

Disney helped put Shia LaBeouf on the map.

The sitcom *Even Stevens* (2000–2003) gave the teenaged actor his first real gig years before he starred in *Transformers*.

The network's animated shows also catered to a slightly older Disney fan.

Less family sitcom and more outwardly fantastical, original cartoons like *Kim Possible* and *Phineas and Ferb* had a goofy, antic-centric quality.

Phineas and Ferb kicked off the newly formed Disney XD in 2009.

After premiering on USA in 2007, the show moved to Disney XD to introduce the channel's mix of sports, movies, and animated shows targeted toward tween boys.

QUIZ

Which of these 2000s stars did *not* get their start on Disney's *The All New Mickey Mouse Club* in the '90s?

A. Ryan Gosling
B. Christina Aguilera
C. Justin Timberlake
D. Justin Bieber

Quiz Answer: D.

Disney created a musical that tweens and teens (and even adults) couldn't resist.

High School Musical, a fizzy PG-rated drama about conflict between teen cliques, drew an unprecedented 8 million viewers to Disney Channel in 2006.

It made stars of Zac Efron and Vanessa Hudgens and created a massive franchise.

It also showed off Disney's talent for finding triple-threat kids who could sing, dance, and act.

Efron didn't actually sing in the first movie.

For reasons unknown, Drew Seeley initially performed Troy Bolton's vocals. But Efron fought to have his voice included in the sequels.

The soundtrack went quadruple platinum.

High School Musical: The Soundtrack was the bestselling album of 2006. And this was a year that included albums by P!nk, Taylor Swift, Justin Timberlake, *and* Beyoncé.

Disney quickly turned *High School Musical* into a $4 billion franchise.

They followed up the original film with *High School Musical 2* (2007), *High School Musical 3: Senior Year* (2008), a sold-out concert tour, and even touring ice shows.

Glee's creators swear they did not take inspiration from *High School Musical*.

Despite those denials, Ryan Murphy's *Glee*—which premiered on Fox in 2009—benefited from *High School Musical*'s success with audiences.

Ryan Murphy wrote glee-club leader Will Schuester with Justin Timberlake in mind.

Timberlake was busy touring at the time, but the show wouldn't have been the same without the multitalented Matthew Morrison in the role.

Brittany's Heather Morris toured with Beyoncé.

The backup dancer had been called in to teach the cast the "Single Ladies" dance routine she'd performed on stage for a year and a half when she was cast as the ditzy-but-lovable Cheerio.

Glee made Lea Michele a household name.

She had gotten buzz for the 2006 Broadway musical *Spring Awakening*, which shared an energetic angst with *Glee*, but the series turned her into a star.

Dianna Agron (Quinn) auditioned for the lead role in *Veronica Mars*.

While the lead went to Kristen Bell, Agron appeared in several season-three episodes as the scheming Jenny Budosh.

In the 2000s, The WB was *the* network for teen drama.

The network cornered this market with soap opera–esque shows like *Dawson's Creek* and *One Tree Hill*, witty comedies like *Gilmore Girls*, and fantasy shows like *Smallville*, *Supernatural*, *Charmed*, and *Buffy the Vampire Slayer*.

The WB merged with UPN in 2006 to become The CW.

The new network made for stronger competition against the majors, kept some of the original networks' bigger shows (*America's Next Top Model*, *Everybody Hates Chris*, *Veronica Mars*, *Supernatural*), and started some hits of its own (*The Vampire Diaries*, *Gossip Girl*).

QUIZ

How old was Lane Kim's Keiko Agena in season one of *Gilmore Girls*?

A. 21
B. 15
C. 26
D. 12

Quiz Answer: C.

Multiple 2000s shows used the Stars Hollow set from *Gilmore Girls*.

You can spot the iconic gazebo and the bones of Luke's Diner in *Ghost Whisperer* (2005), *The Mentalist* (2008), and *Pretty Little Liars* (2010).

Gilmore Girls lost more than one heartthrob to other WB hits.

Chad Michael Murray (Tristan) took the lead as Lucas on *One Tree Hill*, Adam Brody (Dave Rygalski) provided comic relief as Seth in *The O.C.*, and Jared Padalecki (Dean) hunted demons as Sam on *Supernatural*.

Supernatural's Lawrence, Kansas, was actually Vancouver, British Columbia.

The area hosted a number of other 2000s shows, including the far less spooky *Psych*.

Both of _Supernatural_'s leads married CW actresses in 2010.

Jensen Ackles married Danneel Harris (Rachel on *One Tree Hill*) in February, and Jared Padalecki married Genevieve Cortese (Ruby 2.0 on *Supernatural*) in May.

Chad Michael Murray turned down the role of _Supernatural_'s Ryan to play Lucas on _One Tree Hill_.

One Tree Hill creator Mark Schwahn wanted him to play Nathan, but he convinced the producers to let him take the lead instead.

The creators of _The O.C._ cast Peter Gallagher first to draw in an adult audience.

They wanted to send a clear message to viewers that the show was as much about the parents as it was about the steamy teen drama.

The O.C. helped Death Cab for Cutie gain their following.

The indie darlings were Seth's favorite band and even appeared in one episode, launching them into the mainstream.

Adam Brody dated costar Rachel Bilson (Summer) throughout filming.

Of course, he'd famously end up marrying *Gossip Girl* star Leighton Meester.

The O.C. creator Josh Schwartz also brought *Gossip Girl* to the TV-watching masses in 2007.

The premise came from a series of novels by Cecily von Ziegesar, who—having literally come from royalty and attended an elite college prep school on the Upper East Side—took the old advice to "write what you know."

Kristen Bell leveraged the cancellation of *Veronica Mars* into a part on *Gossip Girl*.

The day after *Veronica Mars* was canceled, Bell called the head of The CW and asked to audition for the narrator on the newly green-lit teen drama.

The show's season-one ad campaign scandalized parents.

It leaned into the inappropriateness of what its teens were getting up to with posters showing the characters in sexy entanglements next to quotes from outraged critics. Not surprisingly, the angle worked wonders on teens, helping to make the show a ratings hit in its second season.

QUIZ

Which was *not* a negative blurb used in the *Gossip Girl* ads?

A. "Sexy in all the wrong ways"

B. "Mind-blowingly inappropriate"

C. "Every parent's nightmare"

D. "A nasty piece of work"

Quiz Answer: A.

Dawson's Creek featured the first passionate gay kiss on prime time.

In 2000, Jack (Kerr Smith) kissed Ethan (Andy Kaufman) and brought LGBTQ+ representation into the new millennium.

2003's *Queer Eye for the Straight Guy* was inspired by an overheard conversation.

The future show's producers were at a party, where they heard a woman say to her boyfriend, "Why don't you dress like them?" He responded, "Well, they're gay; they know how to dress."

Queer Eye was the only reason many people knew what Bravo was.

The show was the first bona fide hit for the basic cable network, and it helped Bravo became the launchpad for zeitgeist-y shows like *Project Runway*.

Logo TV was the first cable channel specifically made for queer viewers.

Debuting in 2005, Logo replaced a channel few people knew existed: VH1 MegaHits. One trade magazine called it "a highly unusual move" for cable giant Viacom.

Logo launched *RuPaul's Drag Race* in 2009.

The network featured existing shows that already had a queer audience (*Absolutely Fabulous*, *Buffy the Vampire Slayer*), as well as a mix of reality shows, sitcoms, and docuseries (*365gay News*, *The Big Gay Sketch Show*, *Coming Out Stories*), and *Drag Race* is still going strong (now on MTV) because of it.

Grey's Anatomy (2005) featured one of the first openly bisexual main characters on TV.

Season five (2008–2009) saw Sara Ramirez's Callie Torres struggle with discovering her queer identity before falling for fellow doctor Arizona Robbins.

Creator Shonda Rimes championed diversity's normalcy.

She once said, "I am making TV look like the world looks. Women, people of color, LGBTQ people equal WAY more than 50 percent of the population."

Bokhee's Kathy C. An is a real-life surgical nurse.

The medical professional turned actress has been with the series since its first episode.

QUIZ

Which job has Ben Warren *not* held on *Grey's Anatomy*?

A. Anesthesiologist
B. Surgical resident
C. Firefighter
D. Police officer

Quiz Answer: D.

A favorite character from *Grey's* made Jeffrey Dean Morgan a star.

The actor said he hasn't had to audition for a role since playing Dr. Izzie Stevens's doomed love interest, Denny Duquette.

Kate Walsh's Dr. Addison Montgomery was supposed to appear in only five episodes.

Fans liked her enough that she not only earned a permanent spot on the show but also got her own spin-off: 2007's *Private Practice*.

2004's *Lost* was supposed to be more *Lord of the Flies* than spooky sci-fi mystery.

A Hail Mary attempt by ABC and creators J. J. Abrams and Damon Lindelof to capture the zeitgeist, the show was unlike anything else broadcast networks had tried before.

Michael Keaton was originally cast as Jack Shephard.

The plan was to kill off the hero in the first episode. When the creators decided to keep Jack around, Keaton chose to back out rather than become a series regular.

The show's 2010 ending was controversial, to say the least.

Many misinterpreted the "flash sideways" as showing that the characters were dead all along rather than them *eventually* being reunited in the afterlife.

NBC's *Heroes* (2006) attempted to replicate *Lost*'s sci-fi success.

The premiere episode of the teen-centric superhero drama garnered 14.3 million viewers and received the highest rating of any NBC drama within five years. But the show suffered from diminishing returns.

QUIZ

Which of these philosophers did *not* inspire a character's name on *Lost*?

A. John Stuart Mill

B. David Hume

C. Edmund Burke

D. Jean-Jacques Rousseau

Quiz Answer: A.

Survivor ushered in a new era of reality TV, but it wasn't an original concept.

The late-1990s Swedish series *Expedition: Robinson* (like *Swiss Family Robinson*) had the idea first: throw strangers into a remote tropical location where they are grouped into tribes, compete in challenges, and vote each week on who to kick off the show. The US version just followed suit.

Producer Mark Burnett called it "unscripted drama."

One of the reasons *Survivor* was so instantly popular (besides the gorgeous travelogue camerawork) was the unrelenting competitiveness. The contestants quickly turned themselves into dramatic characters to root for or against.

One in six Americans watched the season-one finale.

The show was a hit from the get-go, turning Burnett into a superstar producer and ensuring that many more competition reality shows would follow.

Burnett's *The Apprentice* (2004) put Donald Trump back in the spotlight.

The onetime real estate mogul had fallen on hard times, but *Apprentice* creators built up his businessman brand for a new kind of competition show that turned "You're fired!" into one of the biggest catchphrases of the decade.

Big Brother was another European import.

The US version launched a little over a month after *Survivor* in 2000, but the original first aired in the Netherlands in 1999.

Yes, the name is a reference to George Orwell's *1984*.

Did it feel like a cheapening of the novel's message about totalitarianism and surveillance? Just a bit.

Contestants weren't given a moment's privacy while in the house.

Viewers could watch what the "houseguests" were doing at all times on a dedicated website.

The Amazing Race took competing for large amounts of money on the road in 2001.

The show was supposed to premiere in the summer, but CBS wisely held it for a bigger fall release once they saw the final product.

QUIZ

Which reality-competition program took the Emmy home in 2010?

A. *American Idol*
B. *RuPaul's Drag Race*
C. *The Voice*
D. *Top Chef*

Quiz Answer: D.

The Primetime Emmys added a new category in 2003: Outstanding Reality-Competition Program.

The Amazing Race claimed the award every year from its inception to 2009.

Who Wants to Marry a Multi-Millionaire? failed to win hearts in 2000.

Fifty women vied for the affection of "multi-millionaire" Rick Rockwell, who turned out to have a history of domestic violence and questionable work history and financials. Winner Darva Conger quickly had the marriage annulled, and the show never aired again.

The Bachelor stuck the landing.

Two years later, creator Mike Fleiss gave the gimmick another go with a simpler concept and, presumably, better vetting of the participants. At its peak in 2002, *The Bachelor* was bringing in around 26 million viewers per episode.

The immediate success of *The Bachelor* spawned spin-offs.

The Bachelorette kicked off in 2003, and the short-lived *Bachelor Pad* (think *Real World/Road Rules: The Challenge*) followed in 2010.

Celebrities got in on the competition frenzy with *Dancing with the Stars* in 2005.

The season-one win—Kelly Monaco over the consistently higher-scored John O'Hurley—caused so much controversy that they held a special rematch (for charity). This time, O'Hurley won.

The Brits did it first.

Dancing with the Stars is the American version of their *Strictly Come Dancing*.

Rom-coms dominated theaters in the 2000s.

From Renée Zellweger in *Bridget Jones's Diary* (2001) and Kate Hudson in *How to Lose a Guy in 10 Days* (2003) to Jennifer Lopez in *The Wedding Planner* (2001), Jennifer Garner in *13 Going on 30* (2004), and more, iconic rom-coms boosted more than one career.

Katherine Heigl brought her drama to the big screen before *27 Dresses*.

In addition to causing a dustup in television by saying her storyline on *Grey's Anatomy* wasn't Emmy-worthy, Heigl created a stir by calling out sexism in her 2007 film *Knocked Up*.

Keira Knightly was barely eighteen years old while filming *Love Actually* (2003).

She was also seventeen when she started filming the *Pirates of the Caribbean* franchise.

Cameron Diaz claimed *The Holiday* (2006) was her most physically taxing film.

And she did *Charlie's Angels* in 2003. But running in heels *and* snow takes a different kind of endurance.

Sandra Bullock turned down Julia Roberts's role in *Valentine's Day* (2010).

The star-studded film had the second-biggest opening for a romantic comedy of the decade, just behind *Sex and the City* (2008), and paid Roberts $11,952 per word. This worked out to $3 million total for 251 words and about 6 minutes of on-screen time.

Ensemble movies also had a moment.

From comedies like *The 40-Year-Old Virgin* (2005) and *The Hangover* (2009) to slightly more suspenseful fare like *Ocean's Eleven* (2001) and *The Italian Job* (2003), films were chock-full of talent.

George Clooney became Hollywood's leading man.

He found his legs as a movie star in the 2000s, doing everything from critic-beloved dramas (2007's *Michael Clayton*) to Coen brothers' comedies (2008's *Burn After Reading*).

QUIZ

What was Gerard Butler before he became an actor?

A. Doctor
B. Lawyer
C. Detective
D. Accountant

Quiz Answer: B.

The *Ocean's* films were his biggest hits.

The three heist flicks, which earned more than $1.1 billion worldwide, led to Clooney commanding $20 million per movie.

Clooney was *People*'s Sexiest Man Alive—for the second time—in 2006.

Having already won in 1997, that put him in the small club of two-time winners that included costar Brad Pitt, who took the honor in 1995 and 2000.

The Notebook (2004) heartthrob Ryan Gosling reportedly turned down the honor multiple times.

Insiders have said he finds the award unserious.

Remakes were big business in the 2000s.

While slashers like *The Texas Chainsaw Massacre* (1974/2003) and *Halloween* (1978/2007) dominated headlines, it was 2004's *The Grudge*—a remake of the Japanese horror film *Ju-On* (2002)—that scared up the most box office cash. It earned over $187 million worldwide.

3:10 to Yuma turned a modest Western into an Oscar contender.

The 1957 original was a solid film, but the 2007 remake starring Russell Crowe and Christian Bale turned it into a gritty, modern epic.

Rob Zombie's *Halloween* gave Michael Myers a tragic backstory to mixed reviews.

Unlike the 1978 original, which left Michael Myers's evil unexplained, the 2007 remake dove deep into his childhood trauma. Some fans loved the psychological depth, while others missed the mystery. Either way, it became the highest-grossing *Halloween* film at the time.

Tim Burton tried to top the twist in 1968's *Planet of the Apes* and failed.

The 2001 reboot made over $350 million worldwide but left audiences baffled with a nonsensical twist ending. Even Burton admitted in interviews he didn't know what it meant.

Burton's *Charlie and the Chocolate Factory* was truer to the book but found its own way to be weird.

The 2005 version stayed closer to Roald Dahl's original text than 1971's *Willy Wonka* but also introduced a deeply unsettling backstory for the chocolatier involving childhood trauma and orthodontic abuse.

The 2005 *War of the Worlds* remake featured real disaster footage that hit close to home.

Steven Spielberg's *War of the Worlds* used footage from 9/11 in its opening scenes—a controversial choice aimed at evoking real-world fear and grounding the alien invasion in contemporary anxiety.

QUIZ

Which aughts remake featured a lead actor from the original film?

A. *The Taking of Pelham 123*

B. *Planet of the Apes*

C. *Death Race*

D. *The Texas Chainsaw Massacre*

Quiz Answer: C.

Star Trek: Nemesis's flop almost ended the franchise in 2002.

Then came J. J. Abrams's 2009 reboot. The Spielberg protégé, *Lost* wunderkind, and *Mission: Impossible III* director was brought on board to get the USS *Enterprise* back to exploring strange new worlds.

James Bond got a refresh in 2005.

The ever-suave Irishman Pierce Brosnan played James Bond in four films between the mid-1990s and early 2000s. Producers decided to reboot the franchise with a younger actor in 2005.

Daniel Craig's golden locks made him a controversial choice to play 007.

In his books, Ian Fleming describes the character as having short, dark hair. For a hot minute, fans were apoplectic, even setting up a website dedicated to the cause: CraigNotBond.com.

Craig beat out a lot of other actors for Bond.

Among the stars who did screen tests for Bond before losing out to Craig were Henry Cavill (*Man of Steel*), Goran Visnjic (*ER*), and Sam Worthington (*Avatar*).

Despite early calls for boycotts, Craig's Bond films were huge hits.

Starting with *Casino Royale* (2006), the movies not only pulled in far bigger numbers than earlier iterations, but they also brought the agent into a rougher, tougher Jason Bourne style of espionage.

QUIZ

Which actor turned down multiple offers to play Bond?

A. Clive Owen

B. Jude Law

C. Ewan McGregor

D. Henry Cavill

Quiz Answer: A.

Contrary to popular belief, Halle Berry was not the first Black "Bond girl."

Before Berry played the role of Jinx in 2002's *Die Another Day*, Gloria Hendry played CIA agent Rosie Carver in 1973's Jamaica-set *Live and Let Die*, and Grace Jones played May Day in 1985's *A View to a Kill*.

Berry *was* the first Black woman to win the Academy Award for Best Actress.

Berry took home the award for her role in *Monster's Ball* (2001).

She made almost no money from the movie.

Berry was paid $100,000 for *Monster's Ball*, but she spent $95,000 on expenses. After the Oscar, though, she was able to command more than $10 million a movie.

Berry also "won" the 2005 Razzie Award for Worst Actress for her role in *Catwoman* (2004).

She became the first Oscar winner ever to attend and accept her Razzie Award in person.

Berry's Storm gave her cred with the comic-book community.

The white-haired mutant who can do wicked things with weather appeared in *X-Men* (2000), *X2: X-Men United* (2003), and *X-Men: The Last Stand* (2006).

Hugh Jackman's Wolverine ushered in a new era of superhero movies.

The Aussie actor wasn't the first choice for the role—Scottish actor Dougray Scott had to bow out after a motorcycle accident—but the franchise wouldn't have been the same without him.

Ian McKellan shot his scenes as Magneto early so he could play Gandalf in *Lord of the Rings* (2001).

Director Bryan Singer rearranged the shooting schedule of *X-Men* (2000) so McKellan could do both.

The leather superhero costumes were as uncomfortable as they looked.

The X-Men outfits were so stiff that it took multiple takes for the actors to get over a two-foot-tall wall.

Sam Raimi's Spider-Man (2002) proved superhero movies could be blockbusters.

The film was the first ever to gross $100 million in its opening weekend alone.

Spider-Man trilogy stars James Franco and Tobey Maguire developed some tension between them.

Franco has said it was his crush on Kirsten Dunst (Maguire's girlfriend at the time) that created friction, but sources have quoted Franco as saying that the two "were cool" by the second film.

Numerous actors auditioned for the lead in *Batman Begins* (2005) just before filming began.

They included Joshua Jackson, Eion Bailey, Hugh Dancy, Billy Crudup, Cillian Murphy, Henry Cavill, Jake Gyllenhaal, and Christian Bale, who landed the role. But director Christopher Nolan liked Cillian Murphy so much that he cast him as Dr. Jonathan Crane (Scarecrow).

That movie and its 2008 follow-up, *The Dark Knight*, gave superhero movies a serious edge.

People actually wrote essays comparing Batman's surveillance of Gotham to tactics used by the George W. Bush administration in the Global War on Terrorism.

The Dark Knight got more Oscar attention than any other superhero movie.

It earned four Academy Award nominations and one win: Best Actor in a Supporting Role for Heath Ledger, awarded posthumously for his work as the Joker.

QUIZ

Which Batman villain was *not* in the Nolan movies?

A. Scarecrow

B. Riddler

C. Catwoman

D. Carmine Falcone

Quiz Answer: B.

Brandon Routh's Superman honored the late Christopher Reeve.

Director Bryan Singer wanted a fresh face for *Superman Returns* (2006), and it didn't hurt that lead actor Brandon Routh had an uncanny resemblance to the original Superman.

Iron Man (2008) and the Marvel Cinematic Universe changed Robert Downey Jr.'s life.

After Downey's stints in prison and multiple rehabs, the actor was persona non grata. But director Jon Favreau knew Downey needed to play Tony Stark and fought the movie execs to make it happen. The franchise breathed new life into Downey's career.

A good chunk of the script was written on the spot.

The actors did a lot of ad-libbing, which suited Downey just fine. Costars Gwyneth Paltrow and Jeff Bridges adapted to Downey's penchant for going off-script.

The gamble paid off—literally.

Iron Man was a surprise blockbuster, earning about half a billion dollars for the MCU and jump-starting the biggest movie franchise of all time, with more than thirty-five movies (and counting) at the time of writing.

Iron Man 2 (2010) debuted at number four at the box office.

It's a good thing, because the movie had to incorporate a number of subplots (like S.H.I.E.L.D.'s involvement) to set up the rest of the MCU.

Edward Norton wasn't a fan of the studio's plans for the Hulk.

The lead in 2008's *The Incredible Hulk* wanted more creative control over the character than the ever-expanding franchise could give him.

Pixar spent the early 2000s creating a successful blueprint for Disney to follow.

Monsters, Inc. (2001), *Finding Nemo* (2003), and *The Incredibles* (2004) fine-tuned the 1990s' Pixar formula of smartly written and genuinely funny family-friendly adventures with big-name actors doing the voicework and at least one guaranteed tearjerker moment.

Sulley (*Monsters Inc.*) had 2.3 million strands of hair that needed to be animated separately.

A single frame could take up to twelve hours to animate.

Disney took the baton in 2006.

The entertainment behemoth, which had been distributing Pixar, bought the outfit for $7.4 billion.

They continued the studio's legacy of great animation and heartwarming films.

The late 2000s saw a run of Pixar movies—*Ratatouille* (2007), *WALL-E* (2008), and *Up* (2009)—whose combination of box office success, critical acclaim, and awards was nearly unparalleled by any movie company before or since.

QUIZ

Which Pixar movie brought its own producers to tears?

A. *Ratatouille*

B. *WALL-E*

C. *Up*

D. *Toy Story 3*

Quiz Answer: C.

WALL-E and EVE are acronyms.

WALL-E stands for Waste Allocation Load Lifter: Earth-Class, while EVE stands for Extra-terrestrial Vegetation Evaluator.

2001 was a big year for wizards.

J. R. R. Tolkien's *The Lord of the Rings: The Fellowship of the Ring* and J. K. Rowling's *Harry Potter and the Sorcerer's Stone* both kicked off wildly popular movie franchises that year.

The Fellowship of the Ring was a surprise success, earning almost $900 million at the box office.

Studios had been trying and failing for decades to adapt Tolkien's trilogy. And with a runtime just shy of three hours, a $100 million budget, and a virtually unknown New Zealander in the director's chair, it was a risk.

They filmed all three LOTR movies simultaneously.

All of the principal photography for *The Fellowship of the Ring*, *The Two Towers*, and *The Return of the King* was shot in a fourteen-month window.

Those fourteen months included replacing a lead actor at the last minute.

Viggo Mortensen replaced Stuart Townsend as filming was just beginning for *The Fellowship of the Ring*.

The sequels were even bigger hits.

The Two Towers (2002) and *The Return of the King* (2003) brought the series' total box office to nearly $3 billion.

The Academy Awards paid attention, too.

The Lord of the Ring series won seventeen out of thirty Oscar nominations.

Around 5,000 boys auditioned for the role of Harry Potter.

Director Chris Columbus had seen Daniel Radcliffe in *David Copperfield* (1999) and said he had a "haunted" quality that made him perfect for the part.

Hagrid's Robbie Coltrane was the first to be cast.

He was joined by an all-star cast of venerable British actors, from *Monty Python*'s John Cleese to Oscar winners like Maggie Smith, John Hurt, Ralph Fiennes, and Gary Oldman.

The first movie took in over $1 billion.

Four of the books had been released by the time the movie premiered, ensuring a large audience of clamoring fans.

Harry Potter movies became an almost annual ritual.

All eight movies (one each for books one through six, and two for book seven) came out between 2001 and 2011.

Unlike LOTR, Harry Potter never won an Oscar.

The series' unofficial designation as "kids' movies" hindered its critical reception.

QUIZ

Which actor did Michael Gambon succeed after his death?

A. Richard Harris

B. Peter O'Toole

C. Ian McKellan

D. Bill Nighy

Quiz Answer: A.

28 Days Later gave zombies a second life.

Before 2002, zombies were known for slow, shuffling dread. Then, *28 Days Later* sprinted onto the scene, unleashing rage-infected humans who could run like track stars. The film didn't just scare audiences—it reinvented the zombie and reanimated the genre.

Resident Evil (2002) became the highest-grossing video game–inspired movie series ever.

With six films by the end of the decade, *Resident Evil* (starring Milla Jovovich) delivered a zombie action-horror hybrid that refused to die.

Dawn of the Dead (2004) launched the careers of two superhero directors.

The 2004 remake of *Dawn of the Dead* revived a horror classic and jump-started the careers of director Zack Snyder (*Man of Steel*, *Justice League*) and James Gunn (*Guardians of the Galaxy*), who wrote the screenplay.

Shaun of the Dead (2004) invented the "zom-com."

The movie played the zombie apocalypse for laughs and emotions and introduced the world to the filmmaking duo of Edgar Wright and Simon Pegg.

Zombieland (2009) was originally going to be a TV series.

The concept of "Zombie Kill of the Week" (which celebrates innovative ways of eliminating the undead) was a holdover from the original script, which was heavily revised for the movie.

Moody vampires entered the undead chat in 2008 with the first *Twilight* movie.

Twilight traded blood and gore for chaste longing, forest frolics, and glittering skin and made over $400 million worldwide thanks to fans of Stephenie Meyer's book series.

Robert Pattinson described *Twilight*'s premiere as "like being hit by a truck."

The actor was shocked by the movie's success, as he thought it would be an offbeat indie film when he took on the project.

The producers almost replaced Taylor Lautner after the first movie.

They worried Lautner didn't look physically imposing enough to play the werewolf version of Jacob in the second installment, *New Moon*. But when they saw that the actor had bulked up with intense workouts and added thirty pounds of muscle, they changed their minds.

The soundtrack was a hit, too.

It went double platinum and launched chart-topping singles like Paramore's "Decode." Even Robert Pattinson—a talented singer, songwriter, and guitarist—contributed songs (under a pseudonym).

QUIZ

Which sport were the Cullens particularly skilled at?

A. Basketball
B. Baseball
C. Football
D. Soccer

Quiz Answer: B.

The 2000s marked the end of the infamous "Curse of the Bambino."

After eighty-six years of baseball heartbreak attributed to Babe "The Bambino" Ruth leaving the Boston Red Sox for their dreaded rivals, the New York Yankees, in 1920, the Boston Red Sox finally won the World Series in 2004.

The real miracle was how the Red Sox got to the Series.

The Red Sox became the first team in MLB history to come back from a 3–0 series deficit, beating the Yankees in the ALCS before sweeping the St. Louis Cardinals.

They had "Moneyball" (aka "sabermetrics") on their side.

Theo Epstein brought the concept, which boils down to using analytics to elevate undervalued players, to the Red Sox when he took over as general manager in 2002.

QUIZ

Which team beat the Yankees in the 2003 World Series?

A. Boston Red Sox
B. Florida Marlins
C. Houston Astros
D. New York Mets

Quiz Answer: B.

The Chicago White Sox ended an even longer drought in 2005.

That October, they dominated the postseason, going 11–1 and sweeping the Houston Astros to win their first World Series since 1917.

Ichiro Suzuki broke a record that stood for eighty-four years.

In 2004, Ichiro set a new MLB single-season hits record with 262 hits, breaking George Sisler's 1920 mark of 257.

Barry Bonds broke the single-season home-run record in 2001, with 73 runs.

The San Francisco Giants' slugger led his team to dominance in the early 2000s. He followed up his 2001 record by breaking Hank Aaron's all-time home run record in 2007: 762 to 755.

His doping controversy overshadowed his achievements.

Law enforcement started investigating a Bay Area laboratory and Bonds's trainer, leading to allegations that Bonds had been using performance-enhancing drugs banned by the MLB. In 2003, he swore under oath he was clean. In 2007, he was indicted for perjury.

His record-breaking home run ball is in the National Baseball Hall of Fame and Museum—with an asterisk.

The scandal kept Bonds himself out of the Hall of Fame, and a vocal group of baseball fans and commentators started calling for an asterisk to be put next to his name in the record books to indicate his steroid use.

Football eclipsed baseball in popularity in the 2000s.

After the steroid scandals, "America's pastime" lost some of its allure. The NFL was ready to pick up the slack.

> **QUIZ**
>
> **What was the total revenue of all NFL teams in 2005?**
>
> **A.** $4.3 billion
>
> **B.** $5.7 billion
>
> **C.** $6.5 billion
>
> **D.** $8.4 billion
>
> Quiz Answer: C.

By the early 2000s, Yahoo! Sports had become a hub for dedicated fantasy football fans.

And, in 2007, ESPN boosted its flagging popularity by going all-in with significant enhancements to its fantasy football coverage.

The NFL went international in 2005 with NFL Fútbol Americano.

That year, the league held its first regular season game on foreign soil: the Arizona Cardinals and San Francisco 49ers played in Mexico City. The game attracted over 100,000 fans—the highest attendance for any regular season NFL game.

The average price of a Superbowl ticket skyrocketed over the decade.

In 2001, it was $522. By 2005, the average price had jumped to $885. And by 2010, fans were looking at close to $1,300 per ticket.

The NFL's rowdy cousin, XFL, debuted in 2001 (and lasted three months).

Whipped up by NBC and wrestling magnate Vince McMahon as a no-holds-barred shot across the bow at the NFL (which McMahon dubbed the "No Fun League"), the XFL featured in-your-face bravado and stunts.

The team names reflected the XFL's rougher image.

They included the Chicago Enforcers, Los Angeles Xtreme, Orlando Rage, and Memphis Maniax, among others.

Player jerseys did the same.

The league let players put pretty much any name they wanted on their jerseys. "Death Blow," "The Truth," and "E-Rupt" all had their fans, but the best-remembered player, hands down, was Rod Smart, whose jersey read "He Hate Me."

The injury count began almost as soon as the league did.

Instead of using a coin toss to see who would receive the ball first, players were instructed to "scramble" for possession. One of the first players to try it separated his shoulder in the fight.

The Los Angeles Lakers dominated basketball in the early 2000s.

With Bulls' coach Phil Jackson and star players Shaquille O'Neal and Kobe Bryant, the Lakers won three back-to-back championships from 2000 to 2002.

The 2003 NBA Draft featured several future superstars.

Fans were introduced to LeBron James (Cleveland Cavaliers), Carmelo Anthony (Denver Nuggets), and Dwyane Wade (Miami Heat).

QUIZ

Which was the only other team to win three championships in the 2000s?

A. Boston Celtics

B. Detroit Pistons

C. Miami Heat

D. San Antonio Spurs

Quiz Answer: D.

The "Malice at the Palace" gave the league a black eye in 2004.

When the Indiana Pacers' Ron Artest fouled Detroit Pistons center Ben Wallace during a game in the Palace at Auburn Hills, Michigan, a Pistons fan tossed a drink at Artest, who charged into the stands, followed by one of his teammates. A player–fan melee erupted that had to be stopped by police and lived on in infamy.

After the fight, the NBA cracked down.

Embarrassed by widely seen footage of the brawl, the league gave out 141 games' worth of suspensions to players involved. They also instituted strict dress codes in the belief that it would improve the images of players.

Tiger Woods became the Michael Jordan of golf.

By the early 2000s, his Q Score (a popularity metric used to evaluate marketability) was equal to the NBA All-Star's.

Woods was a trailblazer in a sport long seen as unwelcoming to non-white players.

Woods described himself as "Cablinasian" on *Oprah* to explain his ethnic makeup of Caucasian, Black, Native American, and Asian.

He created the "Tiger Slam" in 2001.

Woods became the first player to win golf's four top tournaments: the US Open, the Open Championship (British Open), and the PGA Championship in 2000, followed by the Masters in 2001. This feat became known as the "Tiger Slam."

Woods brought golf into the mainstream with brand deals.

In 2000, Nike signed an unheard-of $100 million, five-year endorsement contract with the twenty-four-year-old Woods.

The golfer's personal life eclipsed his professional accomplishments in 2009.

A car crash and rumors of infidelity made him a tabloid target and led to him taking a few years off from golf.

An infamous headbutt defined the decade for soccer.

In the 2006 World Cup final, French legend Zinedine Zidane made headlines for being sent off in extra time in his final professional match for headbutting Italian defender Marco Materazzi in the chest.

Cristiano Ronaldo made his professional debut.

Beginning his career with Portugal's Sporting CP in 2002, he then played for Manchester United for six seasons and ended the decade with Real Madrid.

Real Madrid spent massive amounts of money assembling a superstar team.

In the early 2000s, Real Madrid created the Galácticos, a stacked team featuring David Beckham, Zinedine Zidane, Brazil's Ronaldo, Luis Figo, and more.

The United States had its best men's World Cup finish in decades.

At the 2002 World Cup, the men's national team shocked the world by reaching the quarterfinals—their best finish since 1930. They beat Portugal in the group stage and upset Mexico in the Round of 16 before losing to Germany 1–0 in a hard-fought match.

QUIZ

Who was the highest-scoring goalkeeper of the decade?

A. Rogério Ceni
B. Brad Friedel
C. Gianluigi Buffon
D. Iker Casillas

Quiz Answer: A.

NASCAR became the second-most-watched sport (after pro football).

NASCAR's first big national television contract went into effect in 2001, helping the sport transition from a Daytona Beach phenomenon to a national obsession. In 2005, *Fortune* called it "the fastest growing, best-run sports business in America."

Dale Earnhardt's death shook up the sport that same year.

One of NASCAR's most legendary drivers, "The Intimidator," was killed in a final-lap crash at the Daytona 500 on February 18, prompting a safety overhaul.

Talladega Nights: The Ballad of Ricky Bobby put a spotlight on the sport.

Will Ferrell's 2006 comedy lightly mocks NASCAR culture, but the movie became a cult classic with racing fans.

ESPN's X Games solidified themselves as the main stage for action sports in the 2000s.

In 2006, Travis Pastrana landed the first double backflip on a motocross bike, earning him a perfect score and becoming one of the most jaw-dropping moments in sports. Around the same time, Shaun White was winning medals in both snowboarding and skateboarding.

In 2009, freestyle skier Simon Dumont set a world record for height in the quarter-pipe.

He launched himself 35.5 feet above the 38-foot-tall quarter-pipe, earning the record for highest air. He also crashed hard on landing, but he walked away.

"TWENTY-THREE
IS OLD. IT'S ALMOST
TWENTY-FIVE,
WHICH IS ALMOST
MID-TWENTIES."

—JESSICA SIMPSON

THE PAPARAZZI PARADE

The Celebrities We Obsessed Over

Paris Hilton was the first "It Girl" of the 2000s.

By the time she was eighteen years old, she and younger sister Nicky were being dubbed "the littlest socialites in town" by the *New Yorker*.

Hilton modeled for Donald Trump's agency.

Heir to the Hilton Hotels fortune, Paris Hilton went from teen socialite to model by signing with Donald Trump's agency, T Management, when she turned nineteen.

The Hilton sisters were featured in *Vanity Fair* in September 2000.

The issue included a feature called "Hip-Hop Debs," which described Paris and Nicky as club-hopping, Champagne-sipping, fashionista jet-setters whose lives dripped in fabulosity. It created a fantasy of brand names and all-night parties that would last the decade.

Hilton's debut single, "Stars Are Blind," made the *Billboard* Hot 100.

Although her music career was short-lived, the 2006 reggae-lite bop became a surprise hit.

Hilton hit up the MTV Movie Awards the day before reporting to jail.

She had been sentenced in 2007 to forty-five days in jail for driving with a license suspended after an earlier DUI, but the media-savvy heiress never missed an opportunity to expand her brand.

***The Simple Life* (2003) was made for a slightly different duo.**

Creators originally wanted Paris and her sister Nicky slogging through manure-logged fields in stilettos. When Nicky shied away from the idea, Paris approached a number of friends, landing on a deal with Nicole Richie (daughter of Lionel Richie).

Hilarity ensued for five seasons, thanks in part to Hilton's persona.

Paris built her brand on her ditzy-blonde, Barbie-doll image and whispery vocal fry, but she later revealed it was a character she created.

Paris trademarked her catchphrase, "That's hot," in 2007.

She even sued Hallmark for using it (and won).

QUIZ

How did Hilton react to watching her own death scene in *House of Wax*?

A. Cried
B. Laughed
C. Cheered
D. Left

Quiz Answer: C.

Hilton appeared in twenty-five commercials, shows, and movies in the aughts.

From her cameo in *Zoolander* (2001) and her "burgers and bikinis" ad for Carl's Jr. (2005) to bit parts in hit shows like *Veronica Mars* (2004) and *Supernatural* (2009), Hilton was everywhere.

She died grotesquely in 2005's *House of Wax.*

The scene inspired the movie's "See Paris Die" marketing campaign.

The *New York Post* savaged Paris Hilton, Britney Spears, and Lindsay Lohan.

A 2006 edition of the tabloid featured a photo of the three women labeled "Bimbo Summit," while the accompanying article called them "The 3 Bimbos of the Apocalypse."

Hilton and Lohan had been publicly feuding before the pic appeared.

The former Disney star's acquaintance with the heiress's ex, Stavros Niarchos, sparked heated exchanges via the paparazzi, including Lohan hurling a strong expletive at Hilton.

Hilton and former bestie Nicole Richie were also famously on the outs.

"Nicole knows what she did" was Hilton's explanation at the time.

Paris and Lindsay tried to bury the hatchet that night in 2006.

According to Hilton's 2023 memoir, the pair told the paparazzi that there was nothing to any negative rumors before getting in the car for that infamous shot of the trio leaving a Los Angeles nightclub.

QUIZ

Which of these did the article *not* say the trio was lacking?

A. Clues
B. Cares
C. Underwear
D. Hair extensions

Quiz Answer: D.

Perez Hilton was one of the biggest names in the celebrity-gossip business.

But his real name is actually Mario Armando Lavandeira Jr.

His pen name is a riff on that of a certain socialite as well as a combination of his personal story with Hollywood's.

He once said, "The Perez is me—the outsider, the Latino, the gay. And Hilton is the mainstream."

Hilton's first site was called *PageSixSixSix*.

When the *New York Post*, whose trademark was their Page Six gossip column, threatened legal action, he went looking for a new name.

He launched Perezhilton.com in 2004.

On his site, Hilton blogged almost nonstop in a hyperactive, all-caps style and snarky, combative voice that helped set the tone for the decade. He obsessively tracked certain celebrities (like Paris Hilton and Lindsay Lohan) and rarely had trouble finding something to mock.

He seemed to enjoy being as mean as possible.

The gossip columnist called Britney Spears "stupid" and Jennifer Aniston "sad and desperate," and he assigned childish nicknames to other celebs.

In a rebuke of the decade's take on celebrity gossip, the nasty tone worked.

In 2007, Hilton said his site was getting nearly 9 million page views per day.

Lindsay Lohan kept her *Parent Trap* mojo going into the 2000s.

Freaky Friday (2003) was a massive international success and earned the actress an MTV Movie Award for Best Breakthrough Female.

She helped create one of the most iconic movies of the decade.

Fans have been reciting lines from Tina Fey's *Mean Girls* (2004)—like "On Wednesdays, we wear pink" and "She doesn't even go here"—ever since.

Lohan almost played queen of mean Regina George.

Director Mark Waters thought she was perfect for the role but was afraid they'd struggle to find someone with enough presence to star opposite her and make Cady stand out.

She's the only celeb to have both a Barbie doll and a Bratz doll made in her likeness.

Mattel created a MyScene doll (a Barbie spin-off) for her in 2005, and MGA Entertainment created a collection of *Mean Girls* Bratz dolls for the movie's twentieth anniversary.

Lohan released two studio albums in the mid-2000s.

Her debut album, *Speak* (2004), went platinum, and her 2005 follow-up, *A Little More Personal (Raw)*, went gold.

After *Mean Girls*, Lohan tried to revamp her child-star image for an adult career.

That included making *Maxim*'s "Hot 100" list in 2005 and 2006, topping the list in 2007, and making *FHM*'s "100 Sexiest Women in the World" list in 2007 and 2008.

By 2004, she already had a reputation as a hardcore partier.

Lohan turned eighteen that year and became a regular fixture on the party circuit and in the tabloids.

She went into rehab for the first time in 2007.

She was also arrested multiple times for cocaine possession, DUI, and probation violations.

Her personal struggles weren't the only thing that stalled her career.

Lohan turned down parts in hits like *The Day After Tomorrow* (2004), *Lords of Dogtown* (2005), *Poseidon* (2006), *The Hangover* (2009), and *Veronika Decides to Die* (2009).

QUIZ

Whose photo did Lindsay Lohan recreate in *New York* magazine's 2008 spring fashion edition?

A. Marilyn Monroe

B. Ann-Margret

C. Linda Lovelace

D. Elizabeth Taylor

Quiz Answer: A.

Her work landed her in the hospital three years in a row.

Lohan was treated for exhaustion, heat, and dehydration while filming *Herbie: Fully Loaded* (2005), *Just My Luck* (2006), and *Georgia Rule* (2007).

"Oops!... I Did It Again" set the bar for the decade's pop scene.

Britney Spears's 2000 worldwide hit went platinum seven times over.

It also helped Spears break away from her pristine Disney-kid image.

The imagery and lyrics for the song's video played up then nineteen-year-old Britney's sexuality *just enough*.

She tried her hand at acting.

Her performance in the popular road-trip comedy-drama *Crossroads* (2002) received mostly positive reactions, but she never became a crossover star like ex Justin Timberlake.

The former Mouseketeers made fashion history together in 2001.

Spears and Timberlake's matching denim outfits (aka Canadian tuxedos) at the 2001 American Music Awards continue to live in infamy.

Spears's dating life made headlines as often as her music did.

After ending things with Timberlake in 2002, the singer was photographed with choreographer Wade Robson, Limp Bizkit's Fred Durst, and actors Jared Leto and Colin Farrell (among others).

Kevin Federline wasn't her first husband.

Spears married her childhood friend Jason Alexander at the Little White Wedding Chapel in Las Vegas in 2004. They had the marriage annulled fifty-five hours later.

Spears's second marriage—to Federline—and sanity began to implode in 2006.

That's the year she was spotted partying with Paris Hilton as well as driving with her infant son Sean in her lap instead of in a car seat.

In one of the decade's most indelible moments, she let paparazzi follow her into a salon.

There, she buzzed all her hair off with a set of clippers before going outside and whacking one of the paparazzo's cars with an umbrella.

She entered into a conservatorship in 2007.

The same year Spears split from Federline, judge Reva Goetz named her father, James Spears, and attorney Andrew M. Wallet temporary conservators due to concerns about the singer's mental health. It was meant to last days but lasted thirteen years instead.

Despite all of her issues, the singer's 2009 comeback tour was a hit.

Britney's big top–themed *Circus* tour featuring the Pussycat Dolls was one of the biggest concerts of the year and suggested a possible rehabilitation for Spears.

QUIZ

***Circus* made Spears the youngest female artist to have how many albums debut at No. 1?**

A. Two

B. Three

C. Five

D. Seven

Quiz Answer: C.

Michael Jackson was supposed to be at the World Trade Center on 9/11.

The singer was scheduled to have a meeting at the top of one of the Twin Towers but overslept after staying up late with his mom, Katherine.

He made fresh headlines when he welcomed his third child via surrogate.

In 2002, Jackson introduced the world to his son Prince Michael Jackson II, whom he nicknamed "Blanket" (possibly to avoid confusion with his older son, who was nicknamed "Prince").

Jackson sparked an international outcry when he dangled his infant son out a window.

In 2002, Jackson tried to pull a *Lion King* by holding Blanket over the edge of a Berlin hotel balcony and waving to fans below. He later apologized, calling it a "terrible mistake."

MJ's Neverland Ranch became the site of a 2003 FBI raid.

They confiscated sixteen hard drives but found nothing incriminating,

QUIZ

Which accessory became synonymous with Jackson in his later years?

A. Earrings

B. Handheld fan

C. Surgical mask

D. Beanie

Quiz Answer: C.

Jackson's child-molestation trial dominated headlines in 2005.

The singer arrived at court in pajamas one day and was famously photographed standing on top of his SUV, waving to fans like royalty. He was acquitted on all charges.

The eccentric artist's courtroom fashion became tabloid fodder.

From armbands to military-style jackets to those now-iconic pajamas, MJ's courtroom outfits were dissected like red-carpet looks.

After his trial, Jackson moved to Bahrain to escape the press.

He spent almost a year living as the guest of a royal family member and tried to keep a low profile. (It didn't work.) He even flirted with recording new music there.

He announced a massive comeback tour just months before his death.

In March 2009, MJ revealed the *This Is It* concert series—a fifty-show residency in London scheduled to begin in July. Fans bought out the entire run in minutes. He'd suffer cardiac arrest from an overdose of painkillers just three months later.

His death broke the Internet.

So many people searched for "Michael Jackson" at once on June 25, 2009, that the Internet slowed down by 20 percent and Google feared it was under cyberattack.

Music Television (MTV) pivoted away from music in the 2000s.

Producers filled the channel with original shows like *Jackass* (2000), *The Osbournes* (2002), *Punk'd* (2003), *Viva La Bam* (2003), *Pimp My Ride* (2004), *Run's House* (2005), *The Hills* (2006), *Jersey Shore* (2009), and more.

The last episode of *The Hills* broke the fourth wall.

Though many fans of reality TV realized that much of what they saw was scripted and heavily dictated rather than just organic moments captured on camera, the final episode of *The Hills* in 2010 still created a stir. In the last shot, the camera pulls back to reveal the characters standing on a soundstage.

QUIZ

Who said, "We kinda left everybody with, 'Well, you'll never know what's real and what's fake'"?

A. Brody Jenner

B. Spencer Pratt

C. Lauren Conrad

D. Heidi Montag

Quiz Answer: A.

Punk'd brought together some of the decade's favorite celebrities.

Ashton Kutcher made Beyoncé think she'd knocked over a kids' Christmas tree, Justin Bieber made Taylor Swift think she'd ruined a wedding, and Ashley Tisdale involved Zac Efron in a (fake) robbery.

Family drama was no longer private—it was prime time.

The Osbournes made rock legend Ozzy Osbourne's foul-mouthed family a pop-culture sensation and opened the floodgates for shows like *Run's House*, which followed rapper Joseph "Rev Run" Simmons's life as a dad, and *Meet the Barkers*, which turned blink-182 drummer Travis Barker into America's favorite tattooed stepdad.

Ozzy Osbourne wouldn't watch the show.

The singer admitted in a BBC interview that he was perpetually high while filming.

Newlyweds: Nick and Jessica (2003) was rocky from the start.

Jessica Simpson admitted in her 2020 memoir, *Open Book*, that her dad tried to convince her not to marry Nick Lachey (who asked for a prenup) just minutes before walking her down the aisle.

Cribs created a plethora of memorable moments with peeks inside celebrity homes.

From Kim Kardashian's stripper pole and Ludacris's hallway painted like a swamp to Missy Elliott's Ferrari bed and fish-tank chair, viewers could never anticipate what would come next.

Jersey Shore caught heat from Italian Americans.

Although GTL (gym, tan, laundry) caught on quickly, the show came under fire for their rampant use of another term—the ethnic slur "guido"—in its advertising. MTV issued a non-apology apology and continued to enjoy great ratings.

VH1 followed MTV into the profitable abyss of reality programming.

The network traded music-video blocks for shows like *The Surreal Life* (2004), *Hogan Knows Best* (2005), *Flavor of Love* (2006), *Celebrity Rehab with Dr. Drew* (2008), and *The Cho Show* (2008).

The Surreal Life started out on The WB in 2003.

When The WB dropped the show for not including enough game-style challenges, VH1 scooped it up. The off-the-wall celebrity drama helped set the chaotic tone for the network's new programming.

QUIZ

Which season-one contestant married their significant other in the *Surreal Life* finale?

A. Brande Roderick
B. MC Hammer
C. Vince Neil
D. Corey Feldman

Quiz Answer: D.

Show producers stocked up on alcohol to help create conflict between cast members.

They made sure alcohol was more readily available than food. Mark Cronin, executive producer of *Flavor of Love* and *The Surreal Life,* defended the tactic by saying, "I don't think it's fair to blame a producer for your choices and actions."

Celebrity Rehab with Dr. Drew has a shocking track record.

As of 2024, twelve of the show's participants have died, most from substance abuse.

Rock of Love became VH1's biggest celebreality hit.

On September 30, 2007, the season-one finale of *Rock of Love with Bret Michaels* (in which Poison frontman Bret Michaels searches for love) drew 5.4 million viewers.

Bret Michaels insisted the show be "organic and real."

Before filming began, Michaels told producers, "Please don't script me, 'cuz I'll suck." The result was a show that earned big ratings because viewers believed the drama.

The reunion episode sent Web traffic to VH1.com surging.

After the *Rock of Love* 2 finale aired in April 2008, VH1.com saw more than 1 million unique visitors and more than 1.2 million video streams in 24 hours—a network record at the time.

Hogan Knows Best broke VH1 premiere records.

Premiering July 10, 2005, the show earned the largest audience VH1 had ever drawn for a series premiere.

The Hogan family's real-life drama ended the show.

The series was canceled after four seasons following Nick Hogan's serious car crash and reckless driving charges, Hulk's cheating scandal with daughter Brooke's best friend, and his resulting divorce.

Kim Kardashian's dad was buddies with O. J. Simpson.

Kim got an early taste of tabloid culture when her father, Robert Kardashian, became part of Simpson's criminal defense "dream team" for his 1995 trial. (He had been friends with Simpson since the 1970s.)

Kim's not-so-private romantic life made her famous.

In 2006, Kim was romantically connected to both Nick Lachey and actor/rapper/producer Nick Cannon. But it was the sex tape she made with then-boyfriend Ray J that grabbed the nation's attention when it leaked the next year, in 2007.

She had been making a name for herself as a closet organizer.

Despite their immense privilege, Robert and his wife Kris made it clear they expected their daughters to work for a living. So, Kim found work helping celebrities like Paris Hilton, Serena Williams, and Brandy clean out their closets.

> **QUIZ**
>
> **On which other reality show did Khloé make a brief appearance in 2009?**
>
> **A.** *Dancing with the Stars*
>
> **B.** *Celebrity Apprentice*
>
> **C.** *Celebrity Big Brother*
>
> **D.** *Survivor*
>
> *Quiz Answer: B.*

The budding entrepreneur started a clothing business with her sisters in 2006.

Dash Boutique was a joint Kardashian venture between Kim, Kourtney, and Khloé that did a brisk business in high-end clothes.

The Kardashians wasted no time getting into the celebreality business.

By October 2007, many members of Kim's large family were being followed around by cameras for their new reality show, *Keeping Up with the Kardashians*, produced by Ryan Seacrest.

They weren't the E! network's first choice for a family reality show.

When a show that followed Lindsay Lohan's family didn't come to fruition, Ryan Seacrest quickly pitched the Kardashians as a replacement, describing them as similar to the Osbournes but in Calabasas.

Viewership spiked when the drama did.

Although the initial season received lukewarm ratings, tabloids picking up on relationship tension between Kim and then-boyfriend Reggie Bush pushed things along.

The show gave viewers an inside look at Hollywood's cosmetic culture.

Watching Khloé get laser hair removal, Kris undergo a facelift, and Kim receive Botox injections helped create an open dialogue about cosmetic procedures.

Kris Jenner coined the term "momager."

Jenner worked so hard to brand herself as the Kardashian business matriarch that she eventually trademarked the nickname.

Jennifer Aniston and Brad Pitt's 2000 wedding set the standard for deluxe aughts nuptials.

The July 29, 2000, ceremony in Malibu reportedly cost $1 million (in the 2000s, that was real money) and included fireworks, a "wall of caviar," the *Friends* cast, and Melissa Etheridge.

Pitt guested on *Friends* the year after they married.

The Thanksgiving 2001 episode, "The One with the Rumor," featured Pitt as a former schoolmate of Rachel's who started an "I Hate Rachel Green Club."

The couple built a production company together.

Plan B Entertainment, cofounded by Aniston and Pitt along with producer Brad Grey in 2001, made some of the decade's bigger films, like Tim Burton's *Charlie and the Chocolate Factory* and Martin Scorsese's *The Departed*.

The tabloids wouldn't let up on "baby watch."

Aniston even appeared in a 2004 *SNL* sketch in which paparazzi yelled at her, "When are you going to have a baby?!" The actress later admitted she had been struggling with infertility.

Aniston once said she wasn't sure Pitt was the love of her life.

Three years after their wedding, Aniston questioned a *W* interviewer who asked if Pitt was "the love of her life." She replied, "I don't know. I've never been someone who says, 'He's the love of my life.' He's certainly a big love in my life."

Pitt and Aniston divorced in 2005 amid rumors of an affair.

The married Pitt met Angelina Jolie in 2004 while filming the husband-and-wife-assassin film *Mr. and Mrs. Smith*, and their on-screen chemistry fueled wild speculation.

Jolie was working on changing her bad-girl image at the time.

The actress, who was known for playing sultry temptresses (*Original Sin*), sociopaths (*Girl, Interrupted*), and stylish criminals (*Hackers*), became a Goodwill Ambassador for the United Nations High Commissioner for Refugees (UNHCR) in 2001.

The relationship timelines seemed to cross, and the tabloids ate it up.

Aniston and Pitt announced their separation in January 2005. Aniston filed for divorce that March. By April, "Brangelina" were already out in public, being photographed on a beach in Kenya with Jolie's children.

QUIZ

How much did Pitt and Jolie earn from selling pics of newborn twins Knox and Vivienne to *People* and *Hello!* magazines?

A. $1 million

B. $28 million

C. $4 million

D. $14 million

Quiz Answer: D.

People had vehement opinions about the Pitt-Aniston-Jolie love triangle

In 2005, a Los Angeles boutique started selling T-shirts labeled "Team Jolie" and "Team Aniston."

The 2003 rom-com *Gigli* almost torpedoed two careers.

The movie, in which Ben Affleck plays a mobster with a heart of gold who is paired in a kidnapping scheme with assassin Jennifer Lopez, was panned by critics and audiences alike.

Jersey Girl (2004) director Kevin Smith coined "Bennifer."

Smith gave the world its first romantic portmanteau while the couple worked on the film.

QUIZ

What did the couple say was their paparazzi-related breaking point while planning the wedding?

A. Hiring decoy brides

B. Being chased

C. Helicopters overhead

D. Vendor info leaks

Quiz Answer: A.

The tabloids couldn't get enough of Bennifer.

Lopez and Affleck had seemingly opposite celebrity profiles—"Jenny from the block" was a Bronx-raised ex–Fly Girl dancer who rose to fame playing the Tejano singer Selena, while Affleck was an Irish Boston guy who came up through indie movies. That combination made them irresistible to the paparazzi.

The couple met in early 2002 and were engaged by the end of the year.

They postponed the wedding in fall 2003, just before it was supposed to happen. The actors originally said it was because of all the excessive media hype, but they ended up splitting in January 2004.

J.Lo moved on from Ben quickly.

About six months after breaking up with Affleck, Lopez married singer Marc Anthony. They welcomed twins Emme and Maximilian together in 2008.

Bennifer 2.0 became tabloid official in summer of 2004.

Affleck formed a close friendship with costar Jennifer Garner on the set of their 2003 movie *Daredevil*, but both were partnered up. They got together soon after their respective splits.

The couple met on the set of *Pearl Harbor* in 2000.

At the time, Garner was still married to her first husband, *Felicity* actor Scott Foley.

Garner dated her *Alias* costar Michael Vartan after filing for divorce from Foley in 2004.

Funnily enough, Vartan starred alongside Jennifer Lopez in 2005's *Monster-in-Law*.

Affleck and Garner were in the stands the year the Red Sox broke their losing streak.

They made their first public appearance as a couple at Game 1 of the 2004 World Series. (Coincidence?)

They announced their marriage and their first pregnancy at the same time.

Before the end of the decade, they'd have two girls, Violet and Seraphina, and a boy, Samuel, on the way.

Jennifer Garner once "auditioned" to date Tom Cruise.

According to *Vanity Fair*, Scientology officials trying to find a suitable partner for Cruise had him court Garner, Iranian-born actress Nazanin Boniadi, Scarlett Johansson, Sofía Vergara, and, finally, Katie Holmes.

Cruise and ex-wife Nicole Kidman divorced in 2001, after which she left Scientology.

The 5'11" starlet quipped that another perk of the breakup was being able to wear high heels. (Cruise is reportedly 5'7".)

Next, Cruise dated Cruz (Penelope).

The couple met on the set of the film *Vanilla Sky* in 2000 and went on to date for three years. Some report that her Buddhist beliefs became a sticking point among Scientologists.

Cruise made headlines by jumping up and down on Oprah's couch.

While promoting his movie *War of the Worlds* in May 2005 on *The Oprah Winfrey Show*, Tom Cruise stood on the couch to proclaim his love for then-girlfriend Katie Holmes.

Holmes told *Seventeen* magazine, "I used to think that I was going to marry Tom Cruise."

She was engaged to fellow actor Chris Klein at the time. Six months later, they broke up. She was seen with Cruise soon after.

Cruise and Holmes had a whirlwind romance.

They were together just two months before getting engaged.

Baby Suri arrived on the scene in April 2006.

The newborn didn't make her public debut until October, though, sparking tabloid conspiracy theories that she didn't actually exist.

QUIZ

How long did Mariah Carey and Nick Cannon date before marrying?

A. Two years

B. Five days

C. Six weeks

D. Three months

Quiz Answer: C.

The TomKat wedding was an expensive Italian circus.

The couple tied the knot in November 2006 at a castle in Italy. Andrea Bocelli sang, staff used umbrellas to shield Holmes from the swarming paparazzi, and the whole affair cost around $3 million.

Cruise's best man was Scientology leader David Miscavige.

Holmes's maid of honor was her sister Nancy Blaylock.

A number of Hollywood couples attended the star-studded event.

The guest list included Jennifer Lopez and Marc Anthony, John Travolta and the late Kelly Preston, and David and Victoria Beckham.

Everything Oprah touched turned to gold.

Despite Howard Stern's claim to be "King of All Media," the most powerful and omnipresent figure in early 2000s American media was Oprah Winfrey. As podcaster Jenn White said, Oprah could "turn a book into a bestseller, a product into a trend, and people into stars."

The Oprah Winfrey Show was the top-rated talk show through most of the 2000s.

Instead of creating another tabloid-style daytime talk show, the self-made billionaire and secular guru whipped audiences up into frenzies with surprise gifts and self-help tips.

Winfrey launched *O, The Oprah Magazine* in 2000.

This glossy monthly lifestyle magazine, usually referred to as just "*O*," had a circulation of about 2 million readers in its first year.

"Oprah's Favorite Things" became the gospel for holiday shoppers.

Manufacturers fought to be on Winfrey's must-buy list, which was based on one of the show's most popular segments. The products she swore by ran the gamut from iPods to pajamas and tins of Garrett popcorn.

Winfrey made celebrities of therapist Dr. Phil McGraw and cardiothoracic surgeon Dr. Mehmet Oz.

Both men faced controversy in later years for peddling potentially harmful advice and products.

Martha Stewart went from freshly baked pies to prison food in 2004.

It was quite the headline-grabbing fall from grace for the media mogul and lifestyle expert.

She started the 2000s as America's first self-made female billionaire.

Stewart achieved tycoon status when her company, Martha Stewart Living Omnimedia, went public in 1999.

QUIZ

Stewart met Snoop Dogg during which post-prison project?

A. Ceramics class

B. *The Martha Stewart Show*

C. Community service

D. *The Apprentice: Martha Stewart*

Quiz Answer: B.

Selling her stock in biopharmaceutical company ImClone in 2001 sent up a red flag.

Investigators later charged that Stewart and her stockbroker traded on insider information, avoiding a potential $45,000 loss, and lied about it.

She was sentenced to five months in prison and two years of probation.

Stewart maintained her innocence throughout the six-week trial but lost the case decisively. (It didn't help that a friend testified that Stewart bragged about the insider info.)

Even in prison, Stewart was Stewart.

During her time at the minimum-security Alderson Federal Prison Camp in West Virginia, she did a lot of crochet and ceramics.

Winona Ryder was arrested for shoplifting in 2001.

The *Heathers* actress was convicted of grand theft, fined, and sentenced to three years' probation along with 480 hours of community service.

She appeared to have high-end taste.

Ryder was found guilty of stealing about $5,500 worth of clothes from a Beverly Hills Saks Fifth Avenue, including $80 Donna Karan socks, a $760 Marc Jacobs sweater, and $600 Frederic Fekkai hair adornments.

The six-day trial in 2002 was a magnet for excited tabloids.

They ran headlines like the *New York Post*'s "Winona's Cruel Cut: Bled All Over $795 Bag."

Rumors swirled that the district attorney wanted revenge against the Ryder family.

Years earlier, DA Steve Cooley had gone after LSD pioneer Timothy Leary, who was Winona's godfather.

One of the jurors had an obvious conflict of interest.

Peter Guber, chairman and CEO of Sony Pictures Entertainment—with whom Ryder made *The Age of Innocence*, *Dracula*, and *Little Women*—ruled against her.

Ryder stepped away from acting and moved to San Francisco to decompress.

She considered the debacle a sign of a much-needed break.

Mel Gibson went on a drunken tirade heard 'round the world in 2006.

The *Braveheart* actor was spotted driving erratically on the Pacific Coast Highway in Malibu, California, and charged with driving while under the influence. During the arrest, he unleashed a variety of anti-Semitic invective.

Gibson was sentenced to three years' probation and an alcohol-education program.

In addition to issuing apologies, he sought out meetings with Jewish leaders to help him "discern the appropriate path for healing."

According to Winona Ryder, it wasn't a one-off for Gibson.

In a 2010 interview, she said she had witnessed his behavior firsthand at a party they'd both attended. Gibson reportedly asked if he would get AIDS from speaking to Ryder's gay friend, then he asked Ryder if she was an "oven dodger" (a Holocaust-related slur).

QUIZ

Which legendary producer went to prison in 2009 for murdering his girlfriend?

A. Rick Rubin

B. Dr. Dre

C. Quincy Jones

D. Phil Spector

Quiz Answer: D.

Gibson's talent agency, William Morris Endeavor, dropped him in 2010.

At the time, he was embroiled in a legal battle with then-partner Oksana Grigorieva over domestic-abuse allegations. The actor pleaded no contest to a misdemeanor battery charge.

"I JUST WANT
YOU TO KNOW THAT,
WHEN WE TALK ABOUT WAR,
WE'RE REALLY TALKING
ABOUT PEACE."

—George W. Bush

BREAKING NEWS and VIRAL VIEWS

The Headlines That Defined a Decade

The decade's first presidential election was a nail-biter.

Before the 2000s, political races were fairly uneventful, and everything about the 2000 election indicated it would be the same. But the final decision between George W. Bush and Al Gore came down to the Supreme Court.

George W. Bush ran on a platform of "compassionate conservatism."

The Texas governor branded himself as a moderate Republican who would bring honor and integrity back to the White House after Bill Clinton's sex scandal and subsequent impeachment.

Vice President Al Gore distanced himself from President Clinton by heading to the center.

Although he campaigned on climate change and universal health care—hot-button issues today—Gore was seen as a moderate Democrat.

Lobbyist Ralph Nader threw his hat in the ring for the Green Party.

He was blown out of the water, earning fewer than 3 million votes compared to Bush and Gore's roughly 50 million each.

The numbers for Bush and Gore were so close that people didn't know who won.

That may seem normal now, but it was the first election in 174 years that didn't end with a projected winner on election night.

Gore initially conceded.

He later rescinded his concession.

The VP's team requested a manual recount of ballots in Florida.

Bush's team, unsure of which way a recount would go, sued to stop it. The lawsuits, appeals, and emergency motions took weeks to play out.

Hanging chads became a punch line but were a real problem.

These insufficiently punched bits of ballot paper genuinely made it hard to tell whether a vote was intentional, but late-night talk show hosts and email forwards wasted no time generating "hanging chad" jokes.

Republicans rioted.

On November 22, Republicans launched a boisterous protest at the Miami-Dade County elections office. Their business attire led to people calling the event the "Brooks Brothers riot."

The Supreme Court ended things.

A 5–4 decision stopped the recount process at a point where Bush was ahead, making him the next United States president. He lost the popular vote to Gore but won the Electoral College by one vote.

QUIZ

Who was the last president before Bush to lose the popular vote?

A. Rutherford B. Hayes (1876)

B. Benjamin Harrison (1888)

C. Ronald Reagan (1984)

D. Harry S. Truman (1948)

Quiz Answer: B.

Nightly news shows were the tentpoles of the media ecosystem in the aughts.

The anchors were paid millions, commanded people's attention, and could shift a news cycle in minutes.

News orgs mostly toed the line in the early Bush years.

After 9/11 and the invasions of Iraq and Afghanistan, there was pressure on the media to play down or skip past any criticism of the administration.

Ted Koppel was dragged for paying homage to the dead.

On a special edition of ABC's *Nightline*, "The Fallen," in 2004, anchor Ted Koppel read the names of more than 700 American service members killed in Iraq. Some stations saw the memorial as anti-war and refused to run it.

Dan Rather added a folksy charm.

As the 2004 election dragged on, the CBS anchor delivered several memorable news updates, including, "His lead is as thin as turnip soup" and "We don't know what to do. We don't know whether to wind a watch or bark at the moon."

Rather left CBS in 2005 after forty-four years under a firestorm of criticism from conservatives.

The anchor had reported a story for *60 Minutes II* in 2004 that claimed President George W. Bush missed some service obligations while in the Texas Air National Guard but received preferential treatment.

Jon Stewart changed how people got their news.

Stewart took over *The Daily Show* from Craig Kilborn in 1999 and made it must-see viewing through the aughts and beyond. The mockery helped the medicine go down.

Stewart reshaped the writers' room and the show's tone.

The new host rebuilt the writing team with sharp political satirists like Ben Karlin and David Javerbaum, shifting the show from mild jokes to pointed media critiques.

> **QUIZ**
>
> **On which popular TV show did Stewart make a cameo in 2008?**
>
> **A.** *Psych*
> **B.** *Law and Order*
> **C.** *Breaking Bad*
> **D.** *The Simpsons*
>
> Quiz Answer: D.

The 2000 election helped the show find its footing among traditional networks.

Not long after Stewart came on board, the weeks and weeks of hanging chads, strange legal developments, and partisan wrangling that defined that year's presidential contest provided a kind of absurdity only *The Daily Show* was equipped to deal with.

Stewart was named "America's best talk-show host" in 2001.

Time magazine crowned him the top talk-show host in the country after just two years on *The Daily Show*. They praised his unique synergy of personality and format, calling it a "blessed wedding" that elevated both comedy and commentary.

The devastating terror attacks on 9/11 dominated the news and American lives.

In the wake of the attacks, all major US broadcast networks preempted regular programming and stayed live on air for ninety-three straight hours—the longest uninterrupted news coverage in American television history.

American viewers couldn't look away.

According to Pew Research Center, 63 percent said they couldn't stop watching the coverage.

Designer Milton Glaser updated the 1970s-era "I Heart NY" campaign.

The new one read "I Heart NY More Than Ever," with a small bruise on the heart. His students gave out the posters all over the city.

Saturday Night Live asked Mayor Rudy Guiliani, "Can we be funny?"

Guest-hosting with a group of FDNY firefighters for the season premiere just eighteen days after the attack, Giuliani replied, "Why start now?"

Robert De Niro helped launched the Tribeca Film Festival in 2002.

Looking for a way to rejuvenate downtown Manhattan's shattered economy and spirit, De Niro used his connections to create what would become a major stop on the festival circuit, attracting a half-million attendees.

Politicians started wearing American flag pins on their lapels.

The gesture was rarely seen before 9/11 but became so common afterward that politicians who did not wear the pins were chastised for being anti-American.

More people enlisted in the twelve months after the attack than in any year since.

In a surge of patriotism, 181,510 Americans enlisted in active duty, and 72,908 joined the reserves.

US and British forces launched Operation Enduring Freedom on October 7, 2001.

They bombed Taliban and Al-Qaeda targets across Afghanistan, marking the start of America's longest war.

US forces invaded Iraq on March 20, 2003.

Bush justified the invasion by citing the threat of "weapons of mass destruction" (that later proved nonexistent) and Saddam Hussein's dictatorial rule.

Saddam Hussein hung for his crimes in December 2006.

The US military captured the brutal dictator in hiding in December 2003, and the Iraqi Special Tribunal convicted him of crimes against humanity three years later.

QUIZ

Which food did Republicans try to rename when France refused to join the US invasion of Iraq?

A. Quiche
B. French dip
C. Croissants
D. French fries

Quiz Answer: D.

2004 marked the beginning of truly contentious presidential elections.

The terror attacks on 9/11 and the ongoing conflicts in the Middle East gave the parties and their constituents a lot to fight about.

Bush caught a lot of heat for his bumbling stories, malapropisms, and public gaffes.

Article after article panned the president for things like calling the Italian prime minister "amigo" and creating words like "subliminable" and "misunderestimated."

Democratic opponent John Kerry was known for flip-flopping on policy.

The senator from Massachusetts voted to support the invasion of Iraq in 2002 before ultimately voting against the final funding bill.

His explanation was mocked by both Bush's campaign and *The West Wing*.

Kerry said, "I actually did vote for the $87 billion before I voted against it." In a 2005 episode of the Aaron Sorkin drama titled "Message of the Week," presidential candidate Matt Santos says, "Look, I voted for CAFTA before I voted against it."

Green Party candidate Ralph Nader threw his hat in the ring again.

And he lost again.

Bush won handily.

Unlike in 2000, Bush received about 3 million more votes than Kerry and also won the Electoral College 286 to 251.

The "blogosphere" entered the political chat during the 2004 election.

With newly available platforms for public debate, like WordPress-based blogs, legacy media found themselves competing for attention.

Andrew Sullivan was the OG political blogger.

Having real magazine cred (*The New Republic*, *The Atlantic*) helped the British American pundit launch *The Daily Dish* in 2000. His blog was required reading in the early 2000s.

A blog took down Trent Lott.

Talking Points Memo (one of the earliest liberal political blogs) scored a scoop in 2002 that had been passed over by the mainstream media. The blog published remarks from Lott, in which he defended past segregation policies, resulting in a deluge of criticism and the Republican Senate majority leader's resignation.

Wonkette shook up Washington, DC.

Launched by Gawker Media's Ana Marie Cox in 2004, the blog was like *Page Six* for political insiders. It broke through with news of affairs among staffers, sex-abuse scandals, bribery schemes, and corruption cases. (Cox had a lot of material to work with.)

QUIZ

What name was given to Bush's tongue twisters?

A. Bushisms
B. Dubyas
C. Texanisms
D. Bushers

Quiz Answer: A.

Janet Jackson's 2004 "wardrobe malfunction" made headlines and history.

Jackson and Justin Timberlake were performing his song "Rock Your Body" for the Super Bowl XXXVIII halftime show when Timberlake yanked off a part of Jackson's costume to reveal her right breast covered only by a nipple shield. No one knows whether the moment was planned.

CBS was fined $550,000 by the Federal Communications Commission.

Hundreds of thousands of people complained to the broadcast regulatory agency, which doled out its largest fine to date.

Congress got involved in the chaos.

Following a massive media firestorm, the House of Representatives held a hearing about indecent television programming that largely focused on Jackson's exposure.

Jackson's career suffered, but Timberlake's was fine.

Fallout led to the head of CBS/Viacom, Les Moonves, taking Jackson's music videos off MTV and VH1. She was also cut from the Grammys broadcast after not agreeing to apologize on air for the incident.

QUIZ

Who did *not* perform at a Super Bowl following the incident?

A. Paul McCartney
B. The Rolling Stones
C. Jay-Z
D. Bruce Springsteen

Quiz Answer: C.

New Jersey's Democratic governor resigned in 2004 over an affair.

In August of that year, Jim McGreevey announced that he was gay, he'd had had an affair with a male aide, and he would resign. The governor was trying to head off extortion from the aide, Golan Cipel, who promised to drop his sexual harassment claim for $5 million.

Six-term Republican representative Mark Foley resigned over solicitous emails.

The Florida legislator, who had advocated for stricter punishment for sexual predators, was accused in 2006 of sending explicit messages to at least one teenaged congressional page several years prior.

Republican senator Larry Craig got caught up in a 2007 sting operation.

When arrested by an undercover police officer for allegedly soliciting sex in the restroom at the Minneapolis-St. Paul airport, the Idahoan legislator insisted he was innocently picking up a piece of paper. Craig plead guilty to a lesser misdemeanor charge and opted not to run for reelection.

In 2007, the *National Enquirer* outed former senator John Edwards for having an affair.

The former Democratic vice-presidential and presidential candidate had recently celebrated his thirtieth wedding anniversary with his wife, Elizabeth, who was battling terminal cancer, when news broke of the affair and resulting child.

Jack Abramoff became the face of Washington corruption in the 2000s.

What began as a 2005 lobbying investigation spiraled into a web of fraud, bribery, and even a Florida casino boat company tied to organized crime and a murder. Abramoff ultimately pled guilty to conspiracy and tax evasion, serving nearly four years in federal prison.

He opened a DC restaurant specifically to wine and dine politicians.

In 2002, Abramoff launched the high-end restaurant, Signatures, where lawmakers regularly dined on his dime. The steakhouse became an unofficial hangout for Republican power players.

Abramoff scammed Native American tribes out of millions.

One of Abramoff's most lucrative and notorious schemes involved overcharging Native American tribes for lobbying services tied to their casino operations. He and an associate pocketed more than $66 million.

QUIZ

Which actor played Abramoff in George Hickenlooper's *Casino Jack* (2010)?

A. Johnny Depp
B. Kevin Spacey
C. Sean Penn
D. Christian Bale

Quiz Answer: B.

The scandal triggered a charity cash dump.

After Abramoff's guilty plea in January 2006, lawmakers trying to save face redirected more than $414,000 in political donations tied to him or his clients to charity.

Chandra Levy's disappearance rocked the nation's capital.

The twenty-four-year-old intern at the Federal Bureau of Prisons in Washington, DC, went missing in 2001. Her remains were found in Rock Creek Park in 2002.

DC's Metropolitan Police Department took a hit for their investigation.

The organization was criticized for focusing too intently on California representative Gary Condit as the main suspect as well as for poor evidence handling and inadequate searches.

Condit was never charged for Levy's murder.

The married legislator's only crime was having an affair with Levy. Although he was never charged, he did lose his next primary election.

Laci Peterson disappeared on Christmas Eve 2002 in California.

Authorities found the pregnant woman's remains in the San Francisco Bay. The sensational trial ended in the 2004 conviction of her husband, Scott Peterson, who was sentenced to death in 2005.

It took authorities nine months to find Elizabeth Smart.

This was in spite of the fourteen-year-old being held just eighteen miles from her Salt Lake City home and going on several public outings with her kidnappers, Brian David Mitchell and Wanda Barzee.

"Enron'" became synonymous with "scandal" and "theft" in 2001.

Fortune magazine named the Houston-based energy giant "America's Most Innovative Company" six years running. After the company declared bankruptcy in 2001, the FBI discovered executives had been using shady accounting tricks to keep the company's stock price high while it flailed.

Executives cashed out while employees were stuck.

Top Enron execs sold off their stock before the company collapsed, making millions, while employees' 401(k)s were locked up during the bankruptcy, leaving thousands of people with nothing.

The financial scandal took down a major accounting firm.

Enron's auditor, Arthur Andersen, helped cover up the fraud by shredding documents and signing off on cooked books. The fallout was so severe that Andersen went out of business, and 85,000 people lost their jobs worldwide.

Twenty-two people were convicted, including CEOs Kenneth Lay and Jeffrey Skilling.

The charges ranged from fraud and conspiracy to insider trading and obstruction of justice.

Enron's downfall changed US law.

Public outrage led to the Sarbanes-Oxley Act of 2002, a major overhaul of corporate accountability laws that required tighter auditing standards and better transparency.

Bernie Madoff ran the biggest Ponzi scheme in history throughout the aughts.

He defrauded investors out of an estimated $65 billion by using new investors' money to pay fake returns to earlier investors.

He had been quietly running his New York broker-dealer business since 1960.

As the decades passed, Madoff's investments made a lot of money for his customers, most of whom he brought in as referrals through friends and family.

QUIZ

Before running his Ponzi scheme, what was Bernie Madoff best known for?

A. Hosting a TV show
B. Writing a bestseller
C. Advising US presidents
D. Being chairman of the NASDAQ

Quiz Answer: D.

The 2008 financial crisis made Madoff's fraud too hard to hide.

He was arrested that December after investigators discovered he had been operating a dizzyingly complex global scam, which collapsed once the steady flow of new investors dried up.

His victims ran the gamut.

They included celebrities, small investors, charities, and retirees whose pension funds he managed, leaving many destitute.

Madoff pled guilty to the charges and received a 150-year sentence.

He told the feds, "There is no innocent explanation. I've been running a massive Ponzi scheme."

Vermont legalized civil unions between same-sex couples in 2000.

It was the first brick in the road toward marriage equality.

> **QUIZ**
>
> **Which presidential candidate campaigned on striking down DOMA?**
>
> **A.** Barack Obama
>
> **B.** John McCain
>
> **C.** Hilary Rodham Clinton
>
> **D.** Ralph Nader
>
> *Quiz Answer: A.*

The Defense of Marriage Act (DOMA) stalled marriage equality.

The 1996 federal law recognized only marriages between one man and one woman and allowed states to ignore civil unions performed in other states.

Massachusetts became the first US state to legalize gay marriage.

In 2003, the Massachusetts Supreme Court deemed the state's same-sex marriage ban unconstitutional and legalized same-sex marriage in 2004, setting a precedent for other states to follow.

Marcia Kadish and Tanya McCloskey became America's first legally married same-sex couple.

The women joined hands at Cambridge's city hall on May 17, 2004, the day that same-sex marriage became legal. Seventy-seven more Massachusetts couples did the same later that day.

Iowa, Connecticut, and New Hampshire followed suit before the end of the decade.

California reached marriage equality in 2008 only to then join Alabama, Florida, and Texas in passing a constitutional amendment banning same-sex marriage.

***Lawrence v. Texas* (2003) struck down sodomy laws, which prohibited non-procreative sexual acts, in fourteen states.**

The landmark Supreme Court decision overturned a Texas law, effectively invalidating all remaining anti-sodomy laws in the United States.

"Don't Ask, Don't Tell" led to thousands of military discharges throughout the decade.

The hotly debated law allowed LGBTQ+ people to serve in the military as long as they could successfully hide their sexual preference.

The Patriot Act sparked a fierce debate about civil liberties after 9/11.

Signed into law in October 2001, the act expanded government surveillance powers. It became a major flashpoint between national security and individual rights, especially among civil-liberties advocates who feared profiling and overreach.

The Violence Against Women Act (VAWA) found rare bipartisan support.

Though first passed in 1994, VAWA's 2005 reauthorization expanded protections for victims of domestic and sexual violence, including stronger support for immigrant women and better training for law enforcement.

The 2000 US Census was the first to allow people to select more than one race.

For the first time, multiracial Americans were recognized on a federal level. About 7 million people checked more than one box.

Hurricane Katrina became one of the deadliest storms in US history.

Hurricane Katrina made landfall in New Orleans on August 29, 2005, as a Category 4 storm.

Though not the strongest hurricane ever recorded, its impact was catastrophic.

The storm killed 1,833 people and displaced more than 1.5 million residents, making it the costliest natural disaster in US history at the time.

The real disaster was the failure of flood-protection systems.

More than fifty levees and floodwalls failed, allowing storm surges up to 30 feet high to pour into the city. Entire neighborhoods vanished underwater in a matter of hours.

Thousands were trapped in their homes or on rooftops.

Residents in low-lying areas had no time to evacuate as floodwaters rose. Some cut through their attics to escape rising water, while others climbed onto rooftops with homemade signs begging for rescue.

The government's response (or lack thereof) drew national outrage.

Basic aid took too long to arrive, prompting criticism of FEMA, local officials, and the White House. Many viewed the response as a failure of leadership and compassion.

A magnitude 9.1 undersea earthquake caused a devastating tsunami in 2004.

The quake struck off the coast of the Indonesian island of Sumatra, creating waves up to 30 feet high and killing an estimated 228,000 people across 15 countries.

A 2005 earthquake killed tens of thousands.

On October 8, 2005, a 7.6-magnitude earthquake struck the Kashmir region of Pakistan and India. Death tolls vary, with some sources reporting around 74,000 and others reporting more than 80,000 people killed.

Cyclone Nargis devastated Myanmar in May 2008.

It killed an estimated 138,000 people and destroyed 95 percent of buildings and homes in the Irrawaddy Delta.

QUIZ

For which disasters did the Golden Globes raise money and awareness?

A. Hurricane Katrina

B. Cyclone Nargis

C. The Haiti earthquake

D. The Kashmir earthquake

Quiz Answer: A and C.

China's Sichuan province was rocked by a quake in 2008.

On May 12, 2008, a deadly 7.9-magnitude earthquake hit the area, killing more than 69,000 people, displacing millions, and raising global awareness of building-code failures.

A quake devastated Haiti in 2010.

The 7.0-magnitude earthquake may have killed more than 300,000 people and left more than a million more homeless.

The 2008 presidential election was the decade's most dramatic by far.

Both parties took big swings, making it the longest and costliest presidential election yet, with the highest voter turnout.

Senator John McCain beat out former NYC mayor Rudy Giuliani for the nomination.

Other Republican candidates included party favorites Mike Huckabee, Mitt Romney, and Ron Paul.

Senator Barack Obama won his epic battle against Senator Hillary Rodham Clinton.

Though she ultimately lost the Democratic nomination, Clinton earned 18 million votes, leading her supporters to adopt the rallying cry: "18 million cracks in the glass ceiling."

"Birthers" believed Obama was not American (and therefore ineligible to run).

Conspiracy theories about the Hawaiian native focused on his childhood in Indonesia and his father's Muslim faith. Obama releasing his birth certificate and McCain coming to his defense did little to quell them.

Social media and digital outreach revolutionized fundraising and campaigning.

Obama shattered fundraising records by raising over $500 million through more than 6.5 million donations, 6 million of which were $100 or less, with a grassroots-powered, Internet-driven campaign.

Joe Biden added foreign-policy cred to the Democratic ticket.

Obama's running mate, who had been in the Senate since 1973, brought decades of experience to complement Obama's relative newness on the national stage.

McCain shocked the country with his choice of running mate.

Sarah Palin, the relatively unknown governor of Alaska, was the first female Republican vice-presidential candidate and an instant media sensation.

QUIZ

What did Palin call right-wing women?

A. Mama grizzlies
B. Mavericks
C. Pitbulls
D. Straight talkers

Quiz Answer: A.

Palin's celebrity ended up being more of a hindrance than a help.

Her interviews, particularly with Katie Couric, became viral sensations and *SNL* punch lines in which Tina Fey's impersonation ("I can see Russia from my house!") reached cultural-phenomenon status.

Obama appealed to an increasingly polarized populace with a message of unity and hope.

In an iconic 2004 speech, he proclaimed, "There is not a liberal America and a conservative America. There is the United States of America."

Barack Hussein Obama became America's first Black president in 2008.

He received 69.5 million votes to McCain's nearly 60 million.

Buyers increasingly overlooked smaller starter homes for larger, pricier builds.

Throughout the early 2000s, buying a house was considered a necessary step in building wealth.

Then the bubble began to burst in 2006.

Residential investment and building peaked in mid-2006. By the end of the year, housing prices showed clear signs of collapse (a harbinger of financial meltdown).

Mortgage-backed securities were everywhere—and poorly understood.

Banks and investment firms packaged home loans into bundles called mortgage-backed securities (MBS) and sold them as low-risk investments to financial institutions that should have known better.

QUIZ

What nickname was given to big, new, quickly constructed builds?

A. Money pits
B. McMansions
C. Cookie cutters
D. Starter castles

Quiz Answer: B.

Risky subprime loans fueled the housing-market collapse.

Lenders handed out subprime mortgages to high-risk borrowers, including NINJA ("No Income, No Job, No Assets") borrowers, which increased loan defaults across the market.

More than 3 million US homes entered foreclosure in 2008.

Roughly one in fifty-four households received a filing, devastating entire communities.

The Great Recession of 2008 officially began in December 2007.

Warning signs had been flashing for months, and the worst was yet to come, but that's when the National Bureau of Economic Research officially called it.

The value of entire industries vanished seemingly overnight.

The stock market plunged, trillions of dollars disappeared, and household net worth dropped by 17 percent as banks stopped lending and investors panicked. The Dow lost more than 5,000 points between October 2007 and March 2009.

Unemployment nearly doubled to 10 percent by October 2009.

The US unemployment rate jumped from 4.7 percent in late 2007 to 7.3 percent by the end of 2008, peaking at 10 percent in October 2009 (the highest rate since the early 1980s).

Financial giants fell like dominoes.

Big names like Bear Stearns, Lehman Brothers, and IndyMac Bank failed between 2007 and 2008, triggering a global financial panic and major government bailouts.

The Recovery Act was one of the largest spending bills in US history.

Signed by President Obama in February 2009, the American Recovery and Reinvestment Act pumped $787 billion into the economy through tax cuts, infrastructure, health care, education, and clean energy to help jump-start growth after the financial crisis. It worked.

Europe adopted the euro in 2002.

Although the European Union had agreed to a shared monetary system in 1991 and launched the euro as electronic currency in 1999, euro banknotes and coins didn't hit the streets until January 2002. For a short time, people could use their countries' old currency but would get change in euros.

QUIZ

What did the first person to use euros buy with them?

A. Sneakers

B. Tires

C. Fast food

D. Lychee fruit

Quiz Answer: D.

Other European currencies disappeared as the euro took over.

That included Finland's markka, Spain's peseta, Greece's drachma, Italy's lira, and the Netherlands' guilder.

The transition went surprisingly smoothly.

Changing numerous countries over to a whole new money system on the same day was an incredible feat, and it came with several concerns. Cash shortages were considered a possibility. Strikes were threatened. But things went off without a hitch.

Use of the euro helped fan the flames of an American conspiracy theory.

The creation of a North American Union with a centralized currency became a hot-button issue on the campaign trail for the 2008 presidential election. Entire organizations popped up to oppose the nonexistent policy.

Europe plunged into its worst postwar recession between 2008 and 2009.

The European Union saw the GDP drop 4.2 percent, industrial production fall to levels not seen since the late 1990s, and nearly 10 percent of the workforce unemployed.

China bucked the worldwide recession with record stimulus.

Rather than shrink, China boosted its economy, unveiling a $586 billion stimulus plan in November 2008.

Beijing showed off during the 2008 Olympics.

The opening ceremony at the Bird's Nest (aka the National Stadium) was a four-hour tech spectacle that cost more than $100 million. Directed by Zhang Yimou, it featured 15,000 performers, exactly 2,008 synchronized fou drums, and advanced weather-modification technology to prevent rain.

The "Water Cube" (aka the National Aquatics Center) saw Olympians break twenty-five world records.

They were aided in part by Speedo's futuristic LZR Racer suit (designed using NASA research) and the pool's deeper water and energy-efficient design.

Michael Phelps shattered records with eight golds.

One of his most dramatic wins was a photo-finish victory in the 100-meter butterfly, touching the wall just 0.01 second ahead of Serbia's Milorad Čavić.

The Human Genome Project cracked the "blueprint of life" in 2000.

After a global thirteen-year effort, HGP announced the completion of a rough draft sequence of the human genome (the "blueprint of life"). By 2003, they were able to determine the complete order of all 3 billion base pairs that make up human DNA.

President Bill Clinton celebrated the achievement at the White House.

In a joint appearance with UK prime minister Tony Blair, President Clinton hailed the working draft as a revolution, noting it would transform medicine and the ability to diagnose disease.

It was a breakthrough for law enforcement, too.

Human genomic sequence information revolutionized forensic science, allowing law enforcement to positively identify criminals from tiny amounts of DNA found at crime scenes *and* exonerate those wrongly convicted.

Scientists achieved the first complete sequence of the HIV-1 genome in 2009.

Understanding how the virus worked was a huge step in securing better treatments for it.

We got one step closer to a real-life Jurassic Park in 2005.

Researchers discovered soft tissue in the leg bone of a 68-million-year-old *Tyrannosaurus rex*. It shocked scientists, who previously thought soft tissue couldn't survive for millennia, and it provided a concrete genetic link between dinosaurs and birds.

The International Space Station became permanently crewed in November 2000.

One NASA astronaut and two Russian astronauts—Expedition 1—arrived at the ISS on November 2, 2000, and humanity has maintained a 24/7 presence in space ever since.

The *Columbia* disaster grounded the Space Shuttle fleet in 2003.

On February 1, 2003, Space Shuttle *Columbia* disintegrated upon reentry, claiming the lives of all seven crew members. It triggered a twenty-nine-month grounding of the entire fleet, during which NASA suspended ISS assembly flights and drastically overhauled mission safety procedures.

Pluto got demoted in 2006, sparking global outrage.

On August 24, 2006, the International Astronomical Union (IAU) voted to redefine what a planet is—demoting Pluto to a "dwarf planet" because it was not the "gravitationally dominant" body in its orbital space.

QUIZ

Pluto was the Roman god of what?

A. Water
B. Marriage
C. Death
D. Love

Quiz Answer: C.

The world's biggest and most powerful particle accelerator whirred to life in 2008.

The Large Hadron Collider began smashing particles in a 17-mile tunnel under the France–Switzerland border in 2008, creating temperatures hotter than the sun and confirming the Higgs boson's existence several years later.

"MACARONS ARE
THE GWYNETH PALTROW
OF DESSERTS,
BASICALLY."

—*Megan Garber, The Atlantic*

THAT'S HOT!

Fads, Trends, and Phenomena We Couldn't Resist

The Amazing Adventures of Kavalier & Clay started the decade off strong.

Michael Chabon's debut masterpiece, published in 2000, earned the Pulitzer Prize for Fiction in 2001. Its sweeping tale of friendship, magic, war, and comic-book heroism made it a defining novel of the decade.

Sex, Drugs, and Cocoa Puffs (2003) broke new ground in pop essays.

Chuck Klosterman's collection captured pop-culture obsessions with humor and insight and cemented Klosterman as a leading voice in cultural criticism.

David Mitchell's *Cloud Atlas* (2004) wove six stories across a thousand years.

It dazzled critics, with one writing that it made "almost everything in contemporary fiction look like a squalid straggle."

Stieg Larsson introduced Americans to Nordic crime fiction in 2005.

The Sweden-set Millennium trilogy (*The Girl with the Dragon Tattoo*, *The Girl Who Played with Fire*, and *The Girl Who Kicked the Hornets' Nest*) became global bestsellers and kicked off a wave of interest in Scandinavian thrillers.

Cormac McCarthy made the apocalypse Pulitzer-worthy in 2006.

The author of 1990s' book-club perennials like *All the Pretty Horses* went futuristic for his post-apocalyptic father-son novel *The Road* and won the Pulitzer Prize for Fiction in 2007. It was also snapped up by Oprah's Book Club.

James Frey's memoir *A Million Little Pieces* (2003) sold more than 2 million copies.

The book, a harrowing account of his fight to overcome addiction, was selected for Oprah's Book Club in 2005.

There was just one problem: Frey's book was more fiction than memoir.

Reporters dug around and found inconsistencies in Frey's account, leading to a 2006 exposé arguing that the author invented or exaggerated much of *A Million Little Pieces*.

Frey admitted that he'd originally pitched the book to publishers as a novel.

During his *mea culpa* tour, he went on *The Oprah Winfrey Show*. Winfrey, who had initially defended Frey, told him she felt duped and that he "betrayed millions of readers."

Jonathan Franzen was the first author ever to be disinvited from Oprah's show.

When his Midwest-set family melodrama, *The Corrections* (2001), was chosen for Oprah's Book Club, Franzen cringed and called many of Winfrey's other picks "schmaltzy." She responded by withdrawing an offer for him to appear.

QUIZ

Which of Franzen's books helped him reconcile with Oprah in 2010?

A. *Freedom*

B. *Purity*

C. *Strong Motion*

D. *Farther Away*

Quiz Answer: A.

Jeremiah "Terminator" LeRoy made a splash in publishing.

Author J. T. LeRoy was a Southern teenage runaway who channeled his experiences with abuse and addiction into edgy novels like *The Heart Is Deceitful Above All Things* (2001).

Many celebrities embraced LeRoy as a brave new voice in American fiction.

Lou Reed, Madonna, Winona Ryder, and Courtney Love all expressed their love for the author.

LeRoy's public appearances raised eyebrows.

The author rarely showed up in public. When he did, his shy mumbling and penchant for hiding behind sunglasses and wigs added to the mystique.

Reporters discovered that J. T. LeRoy didn't exist.

"J. T. LeRoy" was actually a creation of Laura Albert, a middle-aged Brooklyn-raised writer whose sister-in-law Savannah Knoop had agreed to pose as LeRoy in public.

QUIZ

What does the *K* in J. K. Rowling stand for?

A. Kimberly
B. Kennedy
C. Karen
D. Kathleen

Quiz Answer: D.

J. K. Rowling's UK publisher asked her to hide her gender.

Bloomsbury feared little boys wouldn't read books written by Joanne Rowling. Because she had no middle name, she used her grandmother's initial for her pen name.

Harry Potter fans flocked to midnight release parties for *Harry Potter and the Goblet of Fire.*

Bookstores hosted major events for the July 31, 2000, release that included costume contests, trivia, face-painting, and plenty of other activities for both kids and adults.

The US publisher ran out of books despite a first printing of 3.8 million copies.

Three million copies sold in the first weekend, and many stores couldn't meet the midnight-release demand.

Rowling planned to kill off Arthur Weasley in *Order of the Phoenix* (2003).

She changed her mind at the last minute after realizing Arthur may have been "the only good father in the whole series."

The manuscripts were notoriously highly guarded to avoid spoilers.

To ensure safety, drafts were sometimes physically flown from Rowling's home in Scotland to the publisher in New York and kept in a locked office.

It was a key plot point for *The Devil Wears Prada* (2006).

Formidable boss Miranda Priestly (Meryl Streep) orders Anne Hathaway's Andrea to find advance copies of the latest Harry Potter book for her daughters—an all but impossible task (that she, of course, nails).

The decade's most compelling young-adult vampire series was written by a Mormon mom.

Stephenie Meyer was a twenty-nine-year-old homemaker with a bachelor's degree in English who had never published anything before securing her three-book deal.

The first *Twilight* book was inspired by a dream and took just three months to write.

Meyer dreamed in June 2003 about two young people talking in the woods—an average girl who'd fallen in love with a handsome, sparkly vampire who wanted to drink her blood. By the end of August, she'd fleshed out their whole story.

Publisher Little, Brown and Company offered Meyer $750,000 in a three-book deal.

It was more than they had ever given to a debut author, but it paid off. *Twilight* (2005) became a bestseller, and altogether, the series sold about 160 million copies worldwide.

QUIZ

What were Twilight fans known as?

A. Bellites
B. Twihards
C. Edwardians
D. Squeegees

Quiz Answer: B.

The series was banned from some schools for being "too racy."

Meyer incorporated her Mormon beliefs into the books: her characters don't drink, do drugs, smoke, use curse words, or have sex. But they do experience quite a bit of sexual tension.

Suzanne Collins came up with the story for *The Hunger Games* while flipping through channels.

When the lines began to blur between reality-TV competitions and coverage of the war in Iraq, Collins had a vision of a young heroine competing for her life in a dystopic America.

She was inspired by the Greek myth of Theseus.

In the myth, a young prince of Athens steps up to stop a lottery that chooses seven boys and seven girls of Crete to face the monstrous Minotaur.

Her books laid the groundwork for the success of more dystopia in the YA market.

Hunger Games' protagonist Katniss leading a revolutionary uprising in *Catching Fire* (2009) and *Mockingjay* (2010) sparked a desire for more in readers, who then turned to *The Maze Runner* (2009) and the Divergent series (2011).

Stephen King initially said he "couldn't stop reading" *The Hunger Games*.

Five years after giving the book a glowing review in 2008, though, he called it a "knock-off" of his 1982 book *The Running Man*.

All three Hunger Games books made the *New York Times* bestseller list.

The first book stayed on the list for more than 260 consecutive weeks.

The first broadly successful e-reader launched in 2007.

A light little tablet with a 6-inch grayscale screen, the first-generation Amazon Kindle retailed for $399. It weighed only about 10 ounces and could hold around 200 e-books.

Sony's e-reader launched before Kindle but never matched its success.

The Sony Librie (2004) was the first mass-market e-reader to use E-Ink technology, but it lacked an integrated store or wireless delivery.

There were about 88,000 e-books for sale on Amazon when the Kindle debuted.

Most were $9.99, about a third of what print hardcover books were going for at the time.

Kindle was dubbed "the iPod of reading."

Wired and other outlets compared the Kindle's impact on books to the iPod's effect on music, focusing on its wireless convenience, disruptive pricing, and seamless content delivery.

The Kindle was an immediate hit.

The first Kindles sold out in just five and a half hours, and Amazon shipped an estimated 500,000 in its debut year.

Kindle titles flew off the virtual shelf.

Kindle users were purchasing 2.6 times more titles than average customers.

Whispernet gave Kindle users free 3G access worldwide.

Early Kindles came with a built-in Sprint EV-DO 3G feature called Whispernet that let readers download books anytime without Wi-Fi, a computer, or a contract.

Kindle 2 debuted in February 2009 with dramatic upgrades.

It sported 2 GB storage (or about 1,100 books), 16-level grayscale display, 20 percent faster page turns, longer battery life, and text-to-speech functionality.

QUIZ

Which famous author's first novella was exclusive to the Kindle Store?

A. Dan Brown

B. Nicholas Sparks

C. J. K. Rowling

D. Stephen King

Quiz Answer: D.

Barnes & Noble launched the Nook in 2009 as a direct challenger to the Kindle.

The original Nook had a unique feature: it combined a 6-inch E-Ink display for reading with a small color touchscreen for navigation. It also allowed users to "lend" e-books to friends for up to fourteen days.

When e-book companies competed, readers won.

The Kindle and Nook rivalry led to more features, better devices, and, most crucially, price wars. When Barnes & Noble cut the Nook's price in mid-2010, Amazon dropped the Kindle's price to $189 only hours later.

Starbucks put a café on nearly every corner in America during the aughts.

In 2000, Starbucks had approximately 3,500 stores around the world, about two-thirds of which were in the United States. By the end of the decade, they were operating over 16,500 locations around the world.

They expanded so rapidly that you could sometimes see one Starbucks while standing in another.

Despite being a punch line among comedians, the chain's ubiquity didn't hurt Starbucks' popularity.

Free Wi-Fi turned the cafés into second offices.

In 2002, Starbucks began offering wireless Internet in partnership with T-Mobile. The move helped transform its cafés into popular spots for working and studying, especially for freelancers and students.

Starbucks changed coffee culture.

Specialty coffee drinks like cappuccinos, lattes, and macchiatos were once considered "niche" or "European." But Starbucks helped make them part of everyday American life.

Other chains adapted to compete.

As the coffee revolution spread, the competition adjusted. In 2003, Dunkin' Donuts felt the pressure and started serving up espresso-based drinks. Even McDonald's followed suit, bringing in better coffee and adding a McCafé line of lattes and cappuccinos to their US menus in 2009.

Starbucks set high standards for corporate ethics.

In 2000, the chain introduced Fair Trade Certified™ coffee (meaning it comes from farmers who use sustainable methods and receive a fair price). In 2005, Starbucks acquired Ethos Water and started donating a portion of sales to clean-water initiatives.

Starbucks launched a coffee-cup quote campaign in 2005.

"The Way I See It" initiative saw a series of thought-provoking quotes printed on Starbucks' cups to "inspire old-fashioned coffeehouse conversations."

The quotes came from writers, scientists, and public figures.

Starbucks tried to mix it up with quotes from movie critic Roger Ebert, singer Josh Groban, activist Gloria Steinem, and more.

QUIZ

Which musician did Starbucks quote as saying, "In the end we're all the same"?

A. Paul McCartney
B. Sara Bareilles
C. Ben Kweller
D. Joni Mitchell

Quiz Answer: C.

The company sparked controversy with a quote from author Armistead Maupin.

In 2005, religious conservative activist group Concerned Women for America criticized Starbucks for including the author in their campaign. Because Maupin was gay, the group believed Starbucks was pushing a "homosexual agenda."

Starbucks added its first blended beverages without coffee or tea in 2002.

The Frappuccino Crème brought four new coffee-free flavors to the menu board: vanilla bean, strawberries and crème, double chocolate chip, and chai crème.

The chain also discovered the magic of seasonal drinks in 2002.

That year, the company introduced its Peppermint Mocha, which was a huge hit, followed by the Caramel Brulée Latte and Gingerbread Latte.

They launched the Pumpkin Spice Latte in 2004.

The chain incorporated the "PSL," as its soon-to-be-addicted fans would call it, into their seasonal menu after a hundred-store test run in 2003. It beat out cranberry white chocolate mocha, honey nut, and maple pecan.

Testers enjoyed lots of pumpkin pie with coffee to figure out what worked.

The "Liquid Lab" employees even brought in fall decorations to get in the mood.

Social media frenzy and panic over rumored shortages helped the drink stay on the menu.

Starbucks, believing they needed to "keep things fresh," considered discontinuing the PSL until Facebook and Twitter arrived in 2006 and love for the flavor went viral.

People demanded new forms of caffeine delivery in the 2000s.

While Starbucks was opening stores on every corner, the US market for energy drinks boomed.

Red Bull, which came to the United States in 1997, gained a cult following.

In 2000, a Los Angeles club owner who saw how much people loved the drink opened a bar inside his club that sold only Red Bull.

"Vodka Red Bull" became *the* nightclub drink of the decade.

The buzzy mix of upper and downer was a nightlife mainstay.

Budweiser joined the trend with Extra (aka "B to the E") in 2005.

It combined beer with caffeine, ginseng, and guarana extract in a slim can. It received consistently negative reviews for taste, but it stuck around for almost three years until being discontinued in the United States.

Monster Energy became gamer fuel.

When this drink hit the market in 2002, it quickly challenged Red Bull for stay-up-all-night market dominance. The trademark tall black cans with slashing green claw marks were intensely marketed through extreme sports, concerts, and gaming.

QUIZ

Which energy drink was big with troops in Afghanistan and Iraq?

A. Rip It
B. 5-Hour Energy
C. Monster
D. Rockstar

Quiz Answer: A.

Mad Men inspired people to look to the past.

Almost immediately after this AMC series about conniving 1960s advertising executive Don Draper started in 2007, a highly influential and dedicated set of fans began mining each episode for trends.

Men's fashion took it up a notch in response.

Men's clothing, which had grown increasingly casual over the years, got a little snazzier after people became enamored of *Mad Men*'s sharp Kennedy-era style: thin ties, crisply tailored suits, and snap-brim hats.

Upscale stores selling everything from clothing to home goods got in on the trend.

Brooks Brothers and Banana Republic launched *Mad Men*–inspired menswear lines. J.Crew introduced the very Draper-esque slim-cut Ludlow Suit, and Waterford Crystal created a *Mad Men* barware collection.

Surprisingly, the show was also a boon for cigarette brands.

Because *Mad Men* was realistic about the prevalence of smoking in the 1960s, most of its characters were constantly puffing away on Lucky Strikes (the subject of a Draper ad campaign in the first episode). The brand saw sales increase over the course of the show.

At the start of the decade, roughly one in four American adults smoked at least one cigarette a week.

The key words in that statistic were "at least," and the percentage was only slightly lower by 2010.

Movies and TV shows didn't reflect a real-life downtrend, though.

Although fewer people smoked during the 2000s than in past decades, the prevalence of characters lighting up cigarettes on-screen stayed the same.

QUIZ

What was the name of Hon Lik's e-cigarette?

A. V2 Cigs
B. NJOY
C. blu
D. Ruyan

Quiz Answer: D.

Movie studios began creating policies around smoking midway through the decade.

After steady lobbying by activists, studios started implementing voluntary policies restricting or banning depictions of on-screen smoking in movies aimed at younger audiences. Warner Bros. was first, in 2005. Others, including Disney, followed.

E-cigarettes entered the US market in 2006.

In 2003, a Chinese pharmacist named Hon Lik invented the first commercially successful e-cigarette, or "vape," a battery-powered device that vaporizes liquid nicotine (and often flavorings), intended to help wean people like himself off cigarettes. It didn't work for him. He became a dual user, both smoking cigarettes and vaping regularly.

Sous vide gained steam with home cooks in the 2000s.

The sous vide (French for "under vacuum") method, which had long been used in professional kitchens, involves sealing food in a plastic bag and cooking it in a precisely controlled water bath.

Acclaimed chef Thomas Keller helped popularize it in 2005.

The French Laundry chef started using sous vide in his kitchen before coauthoring *Under Pressure: Cooking Sous Vide* in 2008, raising awareness of the method on the US culinary scene.

Sous vide made its TV premiere in *Iron Chef America*.

The technique reached mainstream food TV when chef Wylie Dufresne used a sous vide machine (aka immersion circulator) in a battle against Mario Batali during a 2006 episode.

The first home sous vide machine launched in 2009.

The SousVide Supreme, marketed as the first sous vide machine designed for home use, retailed for $449 at launch.

QUIZ

Which celebrity chef debuted her wildly successful show *30-Minute Meals* in 2001?

A. Ree Drummond
B. Rachael Ray
C. Martha Stewart
D. Ina Garten

Quiz Answer: B.

Infomercials made the Magic Bullet a household necessity.

Debuting in the early 2000s, the blender became popular thanks to widespread late-night infomercials. Its compact size, single-serving capacity, and low price made it a hit with consumers.

It wasn't a blender—it was a "nutrition extractor."

Infomercials for the Magic Bullet featured "longevity and nutrition experts" demonstrating how fruits and vegetables could be blended into life-changing smoothies.

The smoothie angle worked.

By 2005, NutriBullet (the company behind the Magic Bullet) had sold more than 3 million units, making it one of the most successful direct-to-consumer kitchen appliances of the decade.

Crock-Pots made a comeback even without aggressive marketing campaigns.

Though the slow cooker gained popularity in the 1970s, sales surged again in the 2000s. By 2009, more than 80 percent of US households owned a slow cooker, likely driven by the need for convenient, budget-friendly meals during the Great Recession.

Keurig machines revolutionized Americans' morning coffee habit in 2006.

Keurig's single-serve coffee machines were initially sold to offices starting in the late 1990s. In 2004, Keurig launched its first home-use model. By 2008, consumers could buy K-Cups in grocery stores across the country.

Fortune called Krispy Kreme the "hottest brand in America" in 2003.

The chain, known for its rolling conveyor belts of hot, fresh glazed doughnuts, expanded from about 140 stores in 2000 to more than 350 stores in 2004.

The company went public in 2000.

Stories about the chain's IPO were being reported by everyone, from morning newscasters, who were excited to now have a Krispy Kreme in their town, to business journalists, who marveled over the stock price's meteoric rise and the addictive nature of their hot "Original Glazed" trademark doughnut.

In 2004 and 2005, Krispy Kreme's stock price collapsed.

The SEC launched investigations into accounting shenanigans.

The 2000s also saw a cereal-bar craze.

Cereal wasn't just for breakfast anymore. In the early 2000s, brands like General Mills launched cereal bars as on-the-go snacks. Meanwhile, actual cereal-themed dessert bars like Treat House and Milk Bar popped up in big cities, remixing childhood favorites with a gourmet twist.

Food trucks went gourmet.

The late 2000s saw a rise in trendy, chef-driven food trucks offering everything from Korean tacos (thanks to Los Angeles's Kogi BBQ in 2008) to artisanal grilled cheese. Social media helped fans track down their favorites in real time.

Everyone got obsessed with "superfoods."

Acai, pomegranate, and goji berries popped up everywhere in the mid-2000s, from smoothie bars to skin care products. Dubbed "superfoods" for their purported health benefits, these ingredients became buzzwords for anyone trying to eat clean—or just market a new drink.

Pinkberry made frozen yogurt a must-have treat in 2005.

That year, Pinkberry opened its first store in West Hollywood, selling South Korean–style frozen yogurt mixed up smoothly in a soft-serve machine and offered with a mix of somewhat healthy toppings that allowed patrons to customize their fro-yo.

QUIZ

Which was *not* a real fro-yo brand in the 2000s?

A. Yogoberry
B. Blue Mango
C. Iceberry
D. Sweet Frog

Quiz Answer: C.

Celebrities helped the brand reach cult status.

Everyone from Oprah Winfrey and Charlize Theron to Paris Hilton, Lindsay Lohan, and the cast of *The Hills* were seen enjoying Pinkberry.

South Korean rival Red Mango came to the United States in 2007.

After their store near UCLA became a hit, they soon opened dozens of others.

Sex and the City put cupcakes and Magnolia Bakery on the map.

The 2000 episode in which Carrie and Miranda enjoy cupcakes from the Greenwich Village shop started a dessert revolution. The bakery even created a "Carrie Cupcake" in honor of the scene.

Soon, entire establishments devoted to cupcakes popped up everywhere.

Like fancy cookie places did in the 1980s (shout-out to Mrs. Fields), cupcake boutiques became markers of upscale urban neighborhoods in the 2000s.

The first Crumbs Bake Shop opened in 2003.

Though it was a full bakery, the oversized cupcakes really caught people's attention. Within a few years, they had dozens of locations across several states.

Sprinkles sold out of everything within three hours of opening their doors.

Considered the world's first cupcake-only bakery, it opened in Beverly Hills in 2005.

Competition shows got in on the trend.

Cupcake Wars premiered on the Food Network in late 2009.

QUIZ

Which celebrity was photographed eating a birthday cupcake solo in 2010?

A. Keanu Reeves

B. Julia Roberts

C. Tom Hanks

D. Leonardo DiCaprio

Quiz Answer: A.

Another portable take on cake started trending in 2008.

In 2008, baking blogger Angie Dudley (aka Bakerella) created the cake pop. Although cake balls already existed, she was the first to add the lollipop stick.

Dudley's pops went viral and made a fan of Martha Stewart.

Stewart invited Dudley to share her creation on the homemaking mogul's TV show, leading Dudley to release a cake-pop cookbook in 2010 that sold about a half-million copies.

The rise of macarons in the United States offered dessert lovers a cupcake alternative.

Cosmopolitan Americans started picking up on the macaron, which made its way from France to chic stateside bakeries and coffee shops in the early 2000s.

Kirsten Dunst's Marie Antoinette whet audiences' appetite for them.

Sofia Coppola's 2006 movie *Marie Antoinette* showed the star munching on pastel-colored macarons throughout, which helped boost their popularity.

Macaron mania spread in the late 2000s.

A character on *Gossip Girl* ate one while taking a bath; *O, the Oprah Magazine* featured them; and Starbucks made them available to the masses.

The 2000s saw the tempting return of the "old-timey" bar.

With names like The Violet Hour, Death & Co, and Milk & Honey, these spots reintroduced a century-old cocktail culture to a new generation using low lighting, antique fixtures, and bartenders with handlebar mustaches and suspenders.

Mixology became a recognized craft.

Though the term "mixologist" had existed for over a century, it gained widespread popularity in the 2000s as bartenders began reviving forgotten techniques, rare ingredients, and precise recipes.

Classic cocktails made a comeback.

Drinks your grandparents might have sipped, like the Manhattan, Old Fashioned, and Sazerac, found new life behind bars that prioritized ingredients, balance, and throwback flair.

Twitter and bar blogs helped the trend explode.

Drink culture went digital in the 2000s. Bartenders posted concoctions online, and cocktail nerds followed along, experimenting at home or hunting down bars that took their ice cubes as seriously as their booze.

The Cosmopolitan became a cultural symbol.

Popularized by *Sex and the City* in the late 1990s, the "Cosmo"—a pink mix of vodka, lime, cranberry juice, and Cointreau—became the must-order drink of the early 2000s.

Major chain restaurants got in on the trend (and killed it).

By the time chains like TGI Fridays introduced sugary variations, like their Pink Punk Cosmo (vodka, cranberry juice, and pineapple juice poured over pink cotton candy), critics declared the trend over.

QUIZ

What was J. D.'s cocktail of choice on *Scrubs*?

A. French 75

B. Appletini

C. Cosmopolitan

D. Sidecar

Quiz Answer: B.

Moscow Mules made a stylish return.

This refreshing 1940s classic made with vodka, ginger beer, and lime came roaring back, helped by its signature copper mug and the rise of Instagram-worthy drinks.

The Mojito went mainstream.

Long popular in its native Cuba, this cocktail of rum, sugar, lime juice, soda, and fresh mint took off in the early 2000s. It even earned a cameo in the 2006 movie version of *Miami Vice*, where two characters take a speedboat from Miami to Havana just for the Mojitos.

The Atkins Diet made low-carb eating enticing.

When Dr. Atkins's *New Diet Revolution* was rereleased in 2002, it became a massive bestseller and helped spark a low-carb craze. The diet emphasized high-protein, high-fat foods while minimizing carbohydrates like bread, pasta, potatoes, and sugar.

By 2004, nearly one in ten Americans were cutting carbs.

Surveys at the time showed that about 9 percent of Americans were on a low-carb diet—most influenced by Atkins—prompting grocery stores and restaurants to release low-carb product lines.

Calories took a back seat to carbs.

Unlike previous diet fads that emphasized calorie counting, Atkins allowed for more generous portions of meats, cheeses, and fats. As long as their carb intake was strictly limited, dieters could still enjoy their favorites.

Celebrities helped boost the diet's visibility.

Jennifer Aniston and Rob Lowe were reportedly among those who adopted low-carb eating during the peak of its popularity.

The Atkins brand went bankrupt in 2005.

Though the diet worked for many in the short term, its long-term restrictions were so extensive that it often became unsustainable. By mid-2005, interest in the diet had plummeted, some Atkins-branded products had been discontinued, and the company had filed for bankruptcy.

The Paleo Diet looked to the distant past for health advice.

Loren Cordain's book *The Paleo Diet* argued that what people ate in the pre-agricultural Paleolithic era (2.5 million to about 10,000 BCE) was healthier than the typical early 2000s diet.

Paleo eaters avoided anything not found in the Stone Age.

That meant cutting out grains, legumes, dairy, refined sugar, and processed foods—all staples introduced after the advent of farming around 10,000 years ago.

QUIZ

Who said, "Nothing tastes as good as skinny feels"?

A. Kate Moss

B. Nicole Richie

C. Tyra Banks

D. Jessica Simpson

Quiz Answer: A.

There were definitely health benefits to eating whole, unprocessed foods.

Paleo gained traction among health enthusiasts for promoting fresh produce and lean proteins and discouraging processed snacks.

The problem was that nobody *really* knew what Paleolithic people ate.

Archaeologists and nutritionists noted that Paleolithic diets likely varied widely by geography and season, making it difficult to define a one-size-fits-all approach.

As with Atkins, people had a hard time sticking to the Paleo Diet.

For one thing, Paleolithic people didn't have coffee or tea.

The 2000s had no shortage of extreme diet fads.

A couple of the decade's eyebrow-raising diets were the Baby Food Diet (self-explanatory) and the Special K Diet (replacing two meals a day with Special K cereal served with low-fat milk).

People tried the Cabbage Soup Diet.

A popular crash diet, it was exactly what it sounds like: consuming cabbage soup to fool your body into thinking it was full while severely limiting other food intake over a week.

Beyoncé swore by the Master Cleanse.

To prepare for her role in *Dreamgirls* (2006), Beyoncé reportedly lost twenty pounds in two weeks with a liquid-only diet of lemon juice, cayenne pepper, maple syrup, and water.

Raw-food devotees ate only plant-based foods that hadn't been heated above 118°F.

Practitioners believed that cooking destroys nutrients. The method gained traction in wellness circles but lacked key nutrients and was—like most fad diets—hard to maintain.

Whole30 was born in 2009 and grew fast on Instagram.

Cofounded by Melissa Urban and then-husband Dallas Hartwig, Whole30 involved eliminating sugar, grains, dairy, alcohol, and legumes for thirty days. Gorgeous pictures of unprocessed platefuls helped it spread across social media.

Gwyneth Paltrow went from actress to wellness guru in the 2000s.

Paltrow became one of the decade's biggest wellness and lifestyle influencers without even having a talk show.

It all started with an email.

In 2008, Paltrow began sending out a weekly newsletter from her kitchen in London. It featured high-end travel and food recommendations, wellness routines, and personal reflections.

That simple newsletter quickly evolved into a wellness empire.

What began as curated recommendations soon expanded into full-blown lifestyle branding under the name Goop. The brand promoted high-end cleanses, herbal detoxes, and advice on emotional health and motherhood. (The infamous jade egg would come later, in the 2010s.)

Goop got its name from a branding tip.

Paltrow was told the most successful Internet companies had names with two Os (think Google). So she placed them between her initials to create Goop.

QUIZ

Which alternative therapy did Paltrow put on full display at the 2004 *Anchorman* movie premiere?

A. Reiki

B. Acupuncture

C. Leeches

D. Cupping

Quiz Answer: D.

The Sudoku craze started in 2005.

That year, most of the major British papers were carrying Sudoku. A May issue of *The Guardian* pronounced that its pull-out was "The only newspaper section with Sudoku on every page!"

The game we know as Sudoku was created in the 1970s.

Dell Puzzles, riffing on an eighteenth-century game called "Latin Squares," turned the game into what they called "Number Place" in the '70s. That game made its way to Japan, where it was tweaked, renamed Sudoku, and reintroduced to the West in the mid-2000s.

The game first appeared in the London *Times* in 2004.

Though the number-grid puzzles had been around for years, a prime spot in this major newspaper helped it gain traction in the new millennium.

Sudoku went *really* big in 2005.

In July 2005, Sky One (a British television network) created a 275-foot-square Sudoku grid—the world's largest—on a hillside in Gloucestershire, England, to advertise their new *Sudoku Live* game show. Residents woke up to the sight in total surprise and discovered it had been designed with environmentally friendly materials that would dissolve within a week.

The first flash mob surprised their audience in June 2003 at a Manhattan Macy's.

More than 130 people showed up individually, asked for help finding a "love rug" for their commune, and then left.

QUIZ

Which TV show featured a well-intentioned flash mob gone wrong in 2010?

A. *The Walking Dead*
B. *Modern Family*
C. *Rizzoli & Isles*
D. *Parenthood*

Quiz Answer: B.

Next, 200 people converged on the Manhattan Hyatt.

They engaged in synchronized applause for 15 seconds before leaving.

***Harper's* magazine writer Bill Wasik created the gatherings as a social experiment.**

Before flash mobs were bespoke dance numbers—even before they were dubbed "flash mobs"—they were Wasik's way of poking fun at people who were eager to conform to a trend.

After a few years' absence, flash mobs came back in force.

When the mobs came back during the late 2000s, they had been transformed into big, choregraphed dance routines that surprised and delighted audiences rather than baffling them.

T-Mobile got in on the fun for a 2009 ad.

The company won TV Ad of the Year at the British Television Advertising Awards for surprising London's Liverpool Street station with a real flash mob of more than 350 dancers.

"BA DA BA BA BA,
I'M LOVIN' IT."

—JUSTIN TIMBERLAKE
FOR MCDONALD'S

THE 2000s JUNK DRAWER

Oddities, Surprises, and Pure Nostalgia

American Girl dolls went from teaching history to ruling the mall in the 2000s.

Creator Pleasant Rowland sold the brand to Mattel in 1998. In the 2000s, the toy company opened stores where fans could get doll makeovers, have tea, and shop in person.

They started selling "Girl of the Year" dolls in 2001.

Unlike the historical dolls, these characters were contemporary girls with unique backstories. They included Lindsey Bergman (2001), the first Jewish doll; Kailey Hopkins (2003), a California surfer girl; and Nicki Fleming (2007), a horse lover from Colorado.

An ex-clothing designer for Mattel's Barbie created Bratz dolls in 2001.

Carter Bryant came up with the idea for an edgier, more fashion-forward, and ethnically diverse line of dolls. Their signature look: oversized lips, dramatic makeup, and crop tops straight out of a tween's dream fashion show.

The original set was four dolls.

Rather than individual Barbies, Bratz came as a set of four. The original crew included Cloe, Jade, Sasha, and Yasmin.

The Bratz dolls hit a chord with consumers.

They made nearly $100 million in their first year and hit $2 billion globally by 2005.

Razor scooters took over sidewalks in 2000.

Originally from Japan, the foldable metal scooters took off after US distributor Carlton Calvin brought them over. Nearly 5 million were sold in the first year alone.

The Razor fad burned bright and fast.

As knockoffs flooded the market, their popularity quickly cooled, though Razor later branched out into electric scooters and hoverboards.

Skip-Its continued to smack into ankles.

An '80s and '90s staple, Skip-It saw a resurgence in the early 2000s thanks to neon colors, sparkles, and a barrage of ads on Nickelodeon. The wearable ankle toy turned playgrounds into personal cardio zones.

Tech Decks let kids skateboard with two fingers.

The ultimate fidget toy, these mini skateboards let kids perform tricks on makeshift obstacle courses made of binders, desks, and their older siblings' textbooks.

QUIZ

What was the name of the game-changing tactical series Nerf launched in 2003?

A. N-Strike

B. Power Nerf

C. Air Tech

D. Ball Blasters

Quiz Answer: A.

Tamagotchis made a comeback in the 2000s.

Bandai revived these digital pets in 2004 with better graphics, new characters, and more features, including the ability for two Tamagotchis to "visit" each other via the infrared "Tamagotchi Connection."

Virtual pets got way plusher with Webkinz in 2005.

Each of these stuffed animals came with a secret code to unlock a virtual version online, where kids could play games, decorate homes, and keep their digital pets healthy. At its peak, Webkinz World had over 2 million active users per month.

Neopets were early Internet-obsession bait.

The site exploded in the early 2000s after adding flash games, virtual currencies, and elaborate lore. Kids spent hours trying to refresh the page for rare "paintbrush" drops.

Petz: Catz and Dogz got a glow-up in 2006.

Creators revamped the long-running PC simulation game that let kids adopt pets that mated, aged, and had personalities. The critters wandered across the desktop, occasionally stealing the cursor or knocking over icons.

Littlest Pet Shop got a digital reboot in the 2000s.

Hasbro relaunched this '90s toy line in 2005 with bobble-headed animals who had their own digital universe. They released more than 3,000 unique pets, fueling an obsessive collector's market among elementary schoolers.

By 2005, Build-A-Bear had given life to more than 50 million fuzzy friends.

The brand had stores in thirteen countries where kids could choose a plush animal, stuff it by hand, and add a "heart" before a helpful associate sewed it shut.

Beanie Babies tried to reclaim their cult status with Beanie Boos.

Ty launched Beanie Boos in 2009, betting on giant glittery eyes instead of investment-grade value. It worked: the toys' soft texture and simple designs made them staples of birthday party gift bags and airport stores.

QUIZ

What huggable "As Seen on TV" toy was on every kid's Christmas list in 2009?

A. Moon Sand

B. Floam

C. Pillow Pets

D. Aqua Dots

Quiz Answer: C.

Robosapien made the dream of owning a robot come true for millions.

Created by a NASA roboticist and released in 2004, this programmable humanoid robot could walk, dance, and throw punches. Robosapien sold over 1.5 million units in its first five months.

Toys "R" Us had to ration their Zhu Zhu Pets in 2009.

People went so crazy for the little battery-powered $8 hamsters that stores like Toys "R" Us had to limit how many customers could buy.

HOTorNOT.com allowed people to feel seen—and judged.

Started in 2000 by a couple of guys who had been arguing about the hotness of a woman they saw on the street, HOTorNOT allowed users to upload pictures of themselves and let the world weigh in. Those with the best ratings earned the rank of "hottest."

The founders asked to be judged themselves.

James Hong and Jim Young placed a three-story billboard outside their San Francisco data center showing each of them naked and holding a sign in front of sensitive areas that displayed their HOTorNOT ratings (3.9 and 4.1, respectively, on a 10-point scale).

Its "Meet Me" feature laid the groundwork for future dating apps.

Users on HOTorNOT could set up a short dating profile, which heavily influenced apps like Tinder.

Like every other popular concept in the 2000s, HOTorNOT became a game show.

Are You Hot? The Search for America's Sexiest People (2003) wasn't officially endorsed by the site's creators, but it did piggyback off their success.

Users used digital cameras to get the perfect angled mirror selfies.

The site was full of pre-cellphone selfies, complete with flash glare, frosted tips, trucker hats, and other iconic 2000s accessories.

Flip phones weren't just phones; they were fashion accessories.

Although they couldn't capture good selfies yet, they did have their advantages. Popular models, such as the Motorola Razr, came in metallic colors like hot pink, baby blue, and champagne gold. People personalized them with rhinestones, bedazzled stickers, and dangly phone charms.

Plastic jewelry was bright, bold, and stackable.

Chunky jelly bracelets, snap bands, and colorful plastic rings were must-haves, especially in neon or glittery finishes. Mood rings also made a big comeback, promising to reveal your emotions (or at least your hand temperature).

QUIZ

Which 2000s heartthrob did *not* rock frosted tips?

A. Milo Ventimiglia
B. Justin Timberlake
C. Mark McGrath
D. Joshua Jackson

Quiz Answer: A.

Body glitter was basically a personality.

In the early 2000s, roll-on glitter gel and shimmer sticks were essential for school dances, mall trips, and casual sparkly chaos. Brands like Bonne Bell and Wet n Wild offered glitter in every pastel color, sometimes with scents like cotton candy or bubble gum.

From butterfly clips to zigzag headbands, early 2000s hair was accessorized to the max.

For guys? Spiky hair with frosted tips and lots of gel, or bandanas à la Fred Durst.

“Fast-casual” restaurants created the perfect happy medium for dining in the aughts.

The term described restaurants that were a step up from fast food without the commitment of sit-down restaurants. They offered quality food, no table service, and a more relaxed atmosphere than places like McDonald’s could offer.

The Great Recession made fast-casual dining even more appealing.

As wallets tightened after the 2008 crash, customers sought affordable meals in comfortable spaces without the price tag of full-service restaurants.

Panera Bread was an early breakout success.

Between 2001 and 2006, the chain opened over a thousand locations, capitalizing on its fresh-baked bread, cozy interiors, and menu full of soups, salads, and sandwiches.

Panera became the go-to study spot.

By 2004, Panera had become the largest provider of free Wi-Fi in the United States, making it a hub for students, freelancers, and casual browsers.

QUIZ

Which was the first national chain restaurant to voluntarily list its calorie counts in 2010?

A. Chipotle
B. Chili’s
C. McDonald’s
D. Panera

Quiz Answer: D.

McDonald's helped bring Chipotle to the masses.

Between 1998 and 2005, McDonald's invested more than $360 million in Chipotle, helping it expand from a small regional chain to hundreds of stores across the United States.

Chipotle went public in 2006.

Its IPO was a hit. Shares doubled on the first day of trading, signaling huge investor confidence in fast-casual dining.

McDonald's left too soon.

The fast-food giant sold part of its stake in Chipotle during the 2006 IPO and was fully divested by the end of that year. If McDonald's had held on until 2024, their investment would have been worth $73.8 billion.

Five Guys challenged Mickey D's with an elevated burger experience.

Founded in 1986, this Virginia-based burger joint exploded in popularity in the 2000s, growing from 6 locations in 2001 to more than 500 by 2009.

Starbucks got into the fast-casual game with an expanded slate of food offerings.

They offered upscale bites like paninis and bistro boxes while upgrading stores into community-style hangouts with soft music, leather chairs, and Wi-Fi.

McDonald's decided they needed a new hook for the new millennium.

Facing its first-ever quarterly loss (–$344 million in Q4 2002) and shuttering 175 underperforming locations, McDonald's bet big on a new jingle.

The inspiration for "I'm Lovin' It" came from Germany.

In 2003, McDonald's partnered with Munich-based Heye & Partner, whose pitch—"*Ich liebe es*" ("I love it")—served as the foundation for the global "I'm Lovin' It" campaign.

It was the first unified global marketing campaign.

McDonald's doesn't do half-measures. So, when they launched their new campaign in 2003, they spent about $1.4 billion to blanket the airwaves with ads in eleven languages.

The jingle was originally performed by Justin Timberlake.

A year into his post-NSYNC solo career, the singer even released "I'm Lovin' It" as a stand-alone single.

Even Beyoncé got in on it.

McDonald's brought Destiny's Child on board in 2005 to belt out that jingle.

Rapper Pusha T claims he wrote the jingle.

Although he did perform a version of it, official credits list ad-agency composers and Pharrell Williams as having written and produced it.

In 2003, McDonald's combined two favorites: breakfast sandwiches and pancakes.

The McGriddle's bacon, scrambled egg, and cheese between two maple-flavored pancakes was an instant winner.

They also created one of the biggest fast-food hits of the decade: the Snack Wrap.

The company launched their famous Snack Wraps in 2006. Made with crispy or grilled chicken, lettuce, cheese, and ranch or honey mustard in a soft tortilla, they were beloved for their low price and portability.

Taco Bell's Crunchwrap Supreme went from limited-time offer to menu mainstay.

Created in 2005 to be a "portable, less messy burrito," the Crunchwrap Supreme layered beef, nacho cheese, lettuce, tomato, and a tostada shell inside a grilled tortilla.

Burger King's Chicken Fries first graced the menu in 2005.

Designed for dippability, these breaded, fried chicken strips shaped like fat French fries became a massive hit—so much so that BK was forced to bring them back due to consumer outrage after discontinuing them in 2012.

QUIZ

Which of these was *not* added to the McDonald's menu in the aughts?

A. Fruit 'N Yogurt Parfait

B. McQueso

C. McPhilly Cheesesteak

D. Chicken Flatbread

Quiz Answer: B.

Subway got the idea for their "$5 Footlong" campaign from a franchisee.

In 2004, the owner of a Miami Subway franchise noticed that his numbers dropped on weekends. He had an idea to sell 12-inch sandwiches for $5 on weekends. Sales ballooned, other franchisees picked up on the idea, and then Subway rolled out the gimmick nationwide in 2008 with the now-iconic "Five ... five dollar ... five-dollar footlong" jingle.

Fanta launched the "Fantanas Invasion" in 2002.

The ad campaign featured the Fantanas, a quartet of brightly dressed women (each repping a different soda flavor), dancing and singing the brand's catchy jingle: "Wanna Fanta? Don't you wanna?"

The original J. G. Wentworth ad was so bizarre that it went viral before "viral" was a thing.

The financial company famous for "structured settlements" aired theatrical commercials in which fully costumed opera singers belted out, "It's my money and I need it now!" with all the gusto of a Puccini aria.

A credit-report ad was the biggest thing French-Canadian singer Eric Violette ever did.

Violette led the band GodAgainstGod, but most people know him as the hapless guy singing the goofy jingles for FreeCreditReport.com. The ads' catchy songs ("F-R-E-E, that spells 'free'!") were instant earworms.

Dove's ad campaigns got "real."

Launched in 2004, Dove's "Campaign for Real Beauty" featured real women of diverse sizes, ages, and ethnicities to challenge beauty standards in advertising. It sparked global conversation and won several industry awards.

Old Spice launched their "The Man Your Man Could Smell Like" campaign in 2010.

Starring Isaiah Mustafa and featuring wild transitions ("I'm on a horse!"), it reshaped ad humor and went wildly viral.

Verizon began asking America, "Can You Hear Me Now?" in 2002.

Paul Marcarelli played the nerdy-yet-dedicated Verizon tech constantly checking signal strength in dozens of ads for the phone company. The line "Can you hear me now? Good." became a cultural staple and was even parodied on *SNL*.

Mazda went "Zoom-Zoom."

Mazda's long-running "Zoom-Zoom" ad campaign, which started in 2000 and featured a whispering child and a rhythmic jingle by Kao Rossman, became one of the most recognizable car slogans of the decade.

QUIZ

Which character from the Geico ads got their own sitcom in 2004?

A. The Caveman
B. The Geico Gecko
C. Maxwell the Pig
D. Chatty Cathy

Quiz Answer: A.

"Never Gonna Give You Up" got a second life in the 2000s.

Rick Astley's 1987 hit single never stopped being amazing, but the Internet rediscovered it in the aughts thanks to a trend called "Rickrolling."

"Rickrolling" started with gamers.

In May 2007, a user on a gaming forum claimed to be posting an advance look at the new game *Grand Theft Auto IV* when, in fact, the link went to Astley's music video.

From there, the prank went viral.

The links and memes spread like wildfire, with celebrities and influencers posting "Never Gonna Give You Up" everywhere under different guises.

Even YouTube got in on it.

For April Fool's Day 2008, every home-page link on the video-sharing site sent users to Astley's deep and soulful crooning.

QUIZ

What did Astley say after being told his song had become a popular meme?

A. "How about that?"

B. "Ugh."

C. "What's a meme?"

D. "Cool!"

Quiz Answer: C.